Uncle Ned's Cabin
and The Lost Cause

**By M.B. Barnes
and Transcribed by Charles W. Locklin
and Doris Tait Locklin**

RoseDog✿Books

PITTSBURGH, PENNSYLVANIA 15222

ISBN: 978-0-8059-8694-5
Library of Congress C6ntrol Number: 2007932425

Printed in the United States of America

First Printing

For information or to order additional books, please write:
RoseDog Books
701 Smithfield St.
Third Floor
Pittsburgh, PA 15222
U.S.A.
1-800-834-1803
www.rosedogbookstore.com

As we opened the trunk, a discovery was made. No one that was a relative at the time the trunk was opened had ever seen the trunk open. My dear Mother-in-law, my spouse's mother, Edna Martin Tait, had the trunk next to her bed as long as my wife can remember. Upon my Mother-in-law passing, my wife, Doris Tait Locklin, and sister-in-law Margaret Tait Wilson, opened the trunk while I observed. As they began to take the trunk's contents out, I noticed they had a series of papers approximately four inches wide and six and one half inches long with a beautiful hand script. I asked to see the papers and as I received them I found page numbers in the upper right corner, so I arranged the pages in order and then began to read them. I informed all that this was a biography of a M. B. Barnes which was written by Mr. Barnes. My wife and sister-in-law told me that their father, Porter Edward Tait Sr., was a distant relative of Mr. Barnes as Mr. Barnes was a brother-in-law to James G. Tait. James G. Tait was married to Adele Barnes (M. B. Barnes sister) and they were the parents of Felix Milton Tait, the father of Porter Edward Tait Sr. These papers were preserved by Porter Edward Sr. and Edna Martin Tait in the trunk for over fifty years.

After informing all relatives about the find of the biography of M. B. Barnes, the papers were given to the youngest daughter, Doris Tait Locklin, of Porter and Edna Tait for safekeeping.

The following pages are the biography of M. B. Barnes as written by M. B. Barnes and transcribed by Charles W. Locklin Jr., the husband of Doris Tait Locklin.

Regards,
Charles W. Locklin Jr.
Doris Tait Locklin

Uncle Ned's Cabin and the Lost Cause

A true history or narrative of incidents and original pencil sketches of scenes and surroundings in the home of a southern planter of south Alabama.

By M. B. Barnes

Preface

As I have said in my introduction, this book contains nothing of a fictitious character, but is a plain unvarnished truthful narrative of incidents in my last life. Such as were known in "antebellum" days and since the war in the homes and surroundings of the former southern slave owner and cotton planter. No one as "Bill Arp" said knows better the nature and characteristics of the negro like the old time slave owner.

The northern people do not know them as we do and many here now cannot understand and appreciate the love and sympathy which existed in former days between a good master and a faithful slave. Since the days of reconstruction soon after the war when the carpetbagger had full sway, we have had no race problem to settle in the south. We will never recognize social equality with the negro in the south. The negro does not want it. They do not even complain of disfranchisement here but seem to be content with their lot "if let well enough alone." If they will take Booker Washington's advice they will be prosperous and happy, but it has been said that some of his students have found their way into the penitentiary occasionally; education does not seem to force them always from crime. I hope the report is not true. They should imitate the honest example of the poor old "Uncle Ned" my father's faithful slave who has "Laid down the shovel and the hoe and gone where the "good niggers" go."

MB Barnes

Dedication

As an evidence of sincere and heartfelt gratitude to my three friends in time of need in days of adversity who being "Friends in need were— friends indeed" when the wheel of fortune or misfortune "went back on me." I hereby dedicate this book To Dr. B. S. Barnes my honored brother of Suggsville, Ala., to my brother-in-law James G. Tait of Wilcox County, and to Dr. H. M. Callien my old friend and companion of Chadwick, Perry County, Alabama.

April 1st, 1903.

Introduction
Uncle Ned's Cabin and the Lost Cause

I will endeavor today for the first time in my life to commence a task in which I have never thought of doing before to wit: writing a book. However, having passed through many trials and vicissitudes of life common to mortal man in this sublunary world incidents and events which have happened to me in my present and past life with environments and surroundings peculiar to me have caused me to write this book. The book Uncle Ned's Cabin and the Lost Cause is named in tender remembrance of an old slave and servant of my father brought from North Carolina in the long, long ago before your humble servant was born. "Uncle Ned" was my father's carpenter. The Lost Cause I propose to represent is myself, having been a sufferer financially in the course of time till the present date from the effects and disastrous ending of a "lost cause." I have been called by those who have known me long and best what is termed a "sure genesis" or a man of original character of wit and humor; not eccentric like John Randolph the great orator and statesman of whom it is said wasted more wit and humor in every day conversation than some men ever had in a life time. He concluded before his death that he was an ignorant man after all and that the more he learned the more he found out he did not know. Making a distinction between knowledge and wisdom, he said that "Knowledge is proud that it knows so much while wisdom is humble that it knows no more."

This book is not intended as a romance or a "fictitious tale founded on stern reality" so often called, but is a plain unvarnished truthful narrative of things which have happened in my past life and events in the home life of a southern cotton planter, my father who was well known in the section of country where he lived in Southern Alabama. It seems a great task to me to remember many reminiscences of the past and many of them at the time which gave me much pleasure seem sad realities of the past to an old man like me to contemplate. My illustrations in the book are pencil sketches of different places and scenes of old negroes, cabins, houses, and animals and entirely original with me; most of them are drawn on paste board paper box tops and entirely from memory of places and things not seen by me in many years and all of them at least over fifty miles away from my present place of residence in another county in Alabama from the place I was born and reared. I will therefore ask the kind reader "Don't view me with a critic's eye but pass my imperfections by large streams from little fountains flow; tall oaks from little acorns grow."

Do as the Indian said "you no like; you no take" and I will merely add by way of an apology that if my book does not strike the fancy of the fastidious reader, than I have written the book and drawn the pictures to suit myself.

Chapter I
Uncle Ned

Uncle Ned, the principal character or hero of my book, has told me while I have often talked with him about old times in North Carolina and of days before I was born at his cabin near our home on my mother's place, that my father Samuel T. Barnes and his cousin Thomas Pugh both of Scotland near Halifax County, North Carolina with two sisters' sons of the Bryan family took shipping from Norfolk Virginia for New Orleans with a view of settling in Louisiana as planters. Uncle Ned said the sea was rough at times on the old sailing ship and the "darkies" would be very sea sick at times and by the time they arrived at the port of New Orleans, that the part of the ship in which they traveled became very filthy at which the Captain became angry and swore most heartily.

I have no information as to the time my father remained in Louisiana but suffice it to say he was very much dissatisfied with the country on account of his health; having chills and fevers continuously while there. I think he remained on some of the bayous there and was at Opelousas church it being perhaps only the semblance of a town at that time. He pulled up stakes and leaving his cousin Tom Pugh in Louisiana (who by the way became very wealthy on bayou Lafourche like all the Pugh family in Louisiana of great wealth so considered among sugar planters.) My father left with his negro property intending to return to North Carolina but passing through Southern Alabama he met many of his friends and acquaintances from North Carolina in Clark County who persuaded him to settle there and he accordingly bought a plantation on Bassett's Creek about two miles from Suggsville, a place settled by a man named Suggs; the first host master there.

My father had as his friends in Clark County Alabama from North Carolina the Wilsons, Calliens, Rivenses, Portises, and Sugar Davis. He met my mother who was Miss Carolina Patterson at Jackson on Bigbee River and they were married and lived there sometime after which they moved to Suggsville. My mother was a grand niece of the original Ben Glover who was her mother's uncle and he was my mother's guardian who came to Jackson from South Carolina. I have heard my father relate circumstances which occurred around him before he was married the last time.

The country was mild and unsettled like all new countries and it was infested with horse thieves. One night he heard his horses charging around and making a noise in the lot. He took his gun and going through the garden which was next to the lot, he saw two men trying to coax the horses with corn to catch them. He spoke out aloud and asked them what they wanted with his horses. They immediately ran and jumping the fence he fired on one man on the fence. They made their escape but he found blood on the fence next morning. It was thought the man was carried off by his friends. Another time my father said he was sitting on the front porch of his house when a man rode up (being no enclosure around it) one night after dark and asked if it was him? He answered that it was. The man immediately flashed a pistol in his face but it did not fire being of the old flint and steel pistol of olden times. He wheeled his horse and fled down the hill towards Jackson. My father jumped for his gun and fired in the direction of the noise made by the horse in the dark, but the man escaped. My father thought it was a man with whom he had a previous difficulty at Suggsville. My father was first married to Miss Keys of Tennessee. He had only one son by his first marriage. He was married quite young. His only son by that marriage was William Keys Barnes, my half brother. He was in the Mexican War and after he returned from Mexico it was supposed he went to California. He never returned. When his mother died my father thought the doctor who attended her killed her by malpractice. He challenged him to mortal combat. My brother Alfred has the old flint and steel dueling pistols he brought to fight him with. The doctor declined to fight. My father caught him in a room afterwards, locked the door to chastise him but the doctor escaped out the window.

UNCLE NED'S CABIN.

Chapter II
Old Uncle Tom

Old Uncle Tom, Uncle Ned's father, was the oldest man of my father's negroes on the plantation. He had three other sons; Moses, Anthony, and Lige. Moses and Anthony were blacksmiths and Lige was foreman of the hoe hands. Aunt Moll, my mother's old cook at one time, was his only daughter. Moses and Anthony did all the blacksmith work for the plantation; making plows, horse shoeing, etc. My father owned many slaves and many acres of land. Old Uncle Tom rode a black mule named "Dick" which he used while hunting up his hogs. He also rode him to the little grist mill called the "little mill" close to home on the branch; the "little mill" with the overshot wheel.

Uncle Tom would go to the "little mill" everyday and grind till noon. The pond would not hold water enough to grind any longer. He would then mount upon "old Dick" and return to the plantation to hunt up his hogs. I remember how he would make the little darkies big enough to help him, shuck corn at the barn. After the corn was shucked, he would put it in a handy place for the young darkies to hand it to him while he would shell it with the corn sheller then it was ready for the "little mill."

Old pony Molett with a young darkie on his back would be mustered into service every day to carry two and a half bushel sacks of corn besides to be ground into meal at the "little mill." It required that much meal every day to supply bread for the plantation. Old Molett was the pony to bring it. All of my brothers from my age down learned to ride on Molett. William Barns my half-brother bought him from a man named Molett and rode him home from Tuscaloosa College when the pony was only four years old.

I have often when a boy run two or three miles over the plantation hunting "Molett" just to ride him perhaps the same distance on Saturday. One day I was trying to make him go fast under the saddle he was quite lazy sometimes and did not wish to go fast. When I whipped him he kicked up his hind feet and threw me over his head onto the road flat on my back in the sand. I cried with pain but mounted "Molett" again.

Mrs. Ewing an old lady in our neighborhood being poor often came to our house and would sometimes complain when she was out of food at home. My father was kind to the poor. The old lady came over one day and said while there; she did not know what she would do for bread for she had no meal at home. My father said nothing and Mrs. Ewing returning home told some one there that Mr. Barnes was the hardest hearted man she ever saw. She said she told him she had no bread at home and he did not say a word. While she was abusing him for his hardness of heart, a negro boy rode up on Molett with a large bag of meal saying that Master sent it to Mrs. Ewing.

The old lady changed her tune immediately, saying "I declare Mr. Barnes is the best man in the world after all. I always knew he was a good man."

Old Molett was like one of the family on the plantation and at home; a riding nag for the convenience of all both black and white. He was sold at the sale after my father's death and passed into other hands. I saw him last at Grove Hill. Old Sam Overstreet rode him to town one day with a bunch of game chickens on board. When I mention my old home, I mean the house my father built and lived in to the day of his death, as well as the one my mother had built the first year of the war after the old house was destroyed by fire. The negroes at the plantation always called my father's house the "great house." It was a fine specimen of the old time southern planters' home in structure and appearance. Several years after my father died I was absent from home at that time and coming home at night I found my mother and her youngest children in a room out in the yard. She had retired for the night. The old house had burnt down. The furniture was saved through the prompt action and kind help of our neighbors, but it caused me to shed tears to see the old house in ruins and ashes. I was compelled to seek lodging elsewhere for the night. My mother called on Uncle Ned and his sons to help build a new home.

ACE OF-
SPADES.

"OLD MOLETT" WITH MEAL FROM "LITTLE MILI

Chapter III
Boyhood Memories

I can just remember my early childhood when my father who was fond of having his friends at his house to have the old fashioned reel dances in which they would dance Virginia reels and cut the "pigeon swing" all night and the next day into another night and "go home with the gals in the morning." I thought they were the "out dancingest people" in the world. Uncle Ned was a ripe scholar on the fiddle then in the prime of life. His favorite piece was "Hop-light-ladies, cakes all dough, never mind the weather so the wind don't blow." Another darkie would strike on the triangle made of iron, three -cornered with a small iron rod, keeping time with the music. The gentlemen all danced in pumps or slipper shoes. Dancing in those days was an accomplishment hard to perform and was certainly very active exercise. They would not only dance, but eat big suppers and dinners in the meantime. It cost something to have such frolics and they seemed to enjoy it hugely.

My father was a plain spoken man, but everybody was treated alike at his house. He did not flatter the rich nor oppress the poor. An honest poor man in his estimation was more respectable than a rich rascal. He was a Mason of high degree and had been master of his lodge, but he did not affiliate with them the latter part of his life because he said there were members in his lodge with whom he would not associate. His request at his death was to be buried with Masonic honors though the "Keystone" of a Royal Arch mason remains on his tombstone to this day. He could not be called aristocratic in every sense being very plain and unassuming. He was never heard to boast of his family origin although he had the best blood in his veins that the old Virginia and North Carolina stock could produce. He always consulted my mother in all matters of important business and never did anything contrary to her advice and judgment; in fact she managed his affairs mostly herself the latter part of his life when his health failed. She was consulted even as to the hiring of overseers at the plantation and he went there but seldom in his latter days. He purchased a tract of pine land on Simmons creek; sixteenth section containing six hundred and forty acres at government sale and built a saw and grist mill just above the ford on the road to Jackson five and a half miles from Suggsville. He went to his mill very often to spend the day taking his dinner with him. He rode his pony, Cricket, which he bequeathed to me to his mill, when he did not go in his buggy, but Cricket was his riding pony.

Cricket was my riding pony for several years after my father died. My pony died at the plantation after he was too old to ride. Simmons Creek is a most beautiful stream of water like all the water in that section running through the pine region. The water is clear and limpid. A dime of grain corn dropped to the bottom can be easily seen lying on the ground in the water on the white sand of the creek. The water is not more than waist deep in places and it is very refreshing for bathing in hot weather. I have often bathed in the creek and in the mill pond when a boy. My father kept an old negro to watch the mill at night and when the sawyer was not there to raise the gate in time of rain or flood as the dam would often break which was very annoying for the hands from the plantation to come to fix and fill up deep holes washed out by the flood when the dam broke Uncle Ned was always the man to do the work.

My mother was a woman of great energy of character. She was naturally quick, bright, and intelligent, but in her early day and time children did not have the facilities of education and advantages given them now. She learned a great deal by constant reading of which she was very fond as well as from observation and contact with intelligent refined persons in the circle of society in which she moved. She always had numbers of servants about home and everything moved in order like clock work. She had in the yard a room called "The work house" in which she had two women to weave cloth for the plantation hands after the thread was made and spun on spools by the spinning machine which was worked by two small darkies who turned the crank of the machine. She would often sit up late reeling thread from the machine after supper on a reel making the thread into hanks to weave on the looms worked by the two women aforesaid.

Dr. Dorsey, a physician and relative of my father made his home at our house at one time long ago and my mother took advantage of his instruction and the opportunity to read his medical books and by that means soon became by practice a good doctor herself.

She had a house built in the yard for sick negroes which was called the "hospital." At home, she would have the negroes who were sick brought from the plantation for medical treatment. She had at one time I remember nineteen cases of bilious fever in the "hospital" and every one of them recovered under her nursing and treatment. Free negroes do not get such treatment now because they do not belong to us. They enjoy the blessing of emancipation and are compelled to look out for medical treatment and everything else themselves.

Besides the old plantation my father owned another called the "Beaver Ruin" place near cedar creek which contained I think about eleven hundred acres of fine black lime land which will produce fifty bushels of corn per acre without much cultivation. Lime land however will rust cotton in its growth when it becomes exhausted or worn with age.

He owned a plantation once above Claiborne on the Alabama River which he exchanged for the "Beaver Ruin" place and it was afterwards sold to Sandy Williams by my oldest brother. It was called the "Sandy Williams" place by our family.

My father let my half_brother William cultivate it until he lost his wife which broke him up and my brother quit farming. My father then owned the old plantation, the "Beaver Ruin" place on which tract the McCollum house stood, his saw and grist mill on Simmons creek and the "little mill" to grind corn near home.

My father always consulted my mother in the employment of Overseers to get good men who would not abuse or be cruel to his negroes. He beside allowing them to enjoy themselves once in a while with having barbecues in summer when the crop was "laid by" about the fourth of July, he would let them dance at home Christmas times. Uncle Ned was the fiddler and negroes danced the old time reel and cut the Pigeon Wing to perfection. They seem to have a better ear for music than white people generally, and they jump high off the floor and shake their feet in a manner peculiar to the negro dancing, while they "cut the pigeon wing." My father always kept up the "fish trap" on the big creek called so because the little creek called Smith's creek ran into Bassett's creek near the "fish trap." The fish trap was built with a rock dam across the creek so as to make a tumbling dam for the water to pour into the trap; built in the shape of a very large wagon body but much larger to hold the fish. The water runs through the bottom of the trap into the stream below the dam. The fish are caught by the water tumbling over the dam into the trap when the creek is rising after a heavy rain or wet spell of weather.

It was fine fun for us to visit the "fish trap" after a rain and see the big catfish come in while we were there but we would always find them in the trap next morning caught during the night. We caught a great many sucker fish which were not good on account of the fine bones in their flesh. Sometimes we would find the "alligator" garfish in the trap which had head and teeth something like the alligator but are not desirable for food except for the negroes. They will eat anything in the way of food.

My father always kept good horses and raised horses, cattle, sheep, and hogs. His smokehouse was always supplied with meat. Spare ribs and backbone in winter and you could see home-made hams hanging up above your head in the smoke house. We had a quarry of white lime rock on our land which made fine chimney work. The smoke house had a pit in the ground floor built of lime rock to build a fire in to smoke the meat.

My father always had an orchard of the best variety of peaches which grew from scions of seed of the finest selection. Those days have past never to return; the halcyon days of my early childhood and youth.

There was a place between the old plantation and saw mill on the road to Jackson which my father bought from a man named Dean. An old school mate of my father named Moran from North Carolina lived there a few years. It seems they went to school to this man's father in North Carolina. Moran was a poor man but having formed mutual attachments for each other at school in their boyhood, he gave Moran a home on his land until he finally move to Louisiana. When a small boy, I would ride "old Molett" over to see John Moran the old man's son. Mrs. Moran would always have nice fried chicken, bread, and butter milk for dinner.

Those good old times for me and if the "Yankees" had let us alone we were the happiest and most prosperous people on earth. No murders and crimes committed by negroes which are so common now a days. No jails, chain gangs, and penitentiaries for them in those days as at the present day. The reader may not appreciate what I feel in regard to such a change in affairs here to date, but it shows we never know when we are happy and even in our childhood we have our troubles and as we grow older they sometimes increase with age. "Man that was born of a woman has few days and full of trouble" and it is as inevitable as the "sparks to fly upward" Josh Billings said: "In a dams sin we all joined in" and "Cain killed Able" because he was not "Abel to Cain him" alas! Too bad. In his almanacs of December 1874, his chronology of the weather says: "now the tender bull frog has frozen up solid, and the wider Stebbins wood pile grows less the old speckle hen sits on spillers so sweet is not the rose for me and have you heard that Deacon Jones has lost a "heffer" and such is life and woodman share that tree."

Our.
Fish–Trap.   (45)
"Bassets" creek
"   "

Chapter IV
Free At Last

My book being a narrative treating of incidents in the home and surroundings of a Southern planter, it will naturally occur to the reader that something should be said in regard to the negro and his characteristics, habits, and instincts, better known to an old time slave owner of "antebellum" days on a southern planter's farm than anywhere else. I do not believe in the doctrine advanced by the Darwin theory of evolution from a monkey to a man, as God, in His divine wisdom, could create ten thousand immortal men as easy as He could create one mortal monkey. The monkey being an animal without a soul could not be transformed into an immortal being without interfering very maternally with previous arrangements of animal creation. The monkey may be the connecting link between the animal and man and if so, the negro might come in for his share of the evolution, but Sam Jones says in his book that "the four legged monkey" will not "evolute." The negro takes pattern after the ape family in trying to imitate white people more especially since they have become free.

Perhaps being thrown on their own responsibility they try to imitate people whom they know and feel to be their superiors in intelligence and in every other aspect except for the performance of hard labor in the hot sun so much felt in southern climate in the summer months. They can withstand excessive heat better than a white man and can lie down in the sun for that matter and sleep with the sun shinning in their faces. Their religion is more like superstition than otherwise. They think for instance that it is a great sin for a member of the church to play music on the fiddle or to whistle an old reel, but no harm to lie or steal.

Some of them would steal going home from church without any compunction of conscience whatever. They have but little virtue and I heard of one who is considered an intelligent prosperous negro ask a man what was meant by adultery? If you educate them it destroys their inclination or capacity for manual labor and their ambition is to teach school or preach and the emancipation of the negro of course makes them free and more indolent, idle, and dissolute and being ignorant and of degraded instincts and passions, they have committed brutal crimes in the south which had to be dealt with by severe measures of lynching or which the people at the north make great complaint when they have resorted to lynching and circumstancces at the north.

Desperate crimes require desperate remedies or punishment and it will continue in force as long as such crimes are committed in any civilized community or country. It is a mistake however to think that they are all alike in disposition in that particular and while they are generally alike in their instincts you will find some of them kind, reliable, and trustworthy. The old time darkie like Uncle Ned will have soon passed away. No one can appreciate the existence of the attachment between master and trusty slave in old "antebellum" days like those who once owned these negroes since they have become free and (like the white man compelled to take care of themselves) do not like to pay debts as a general thing for if they think that you do not need it and that white people always have more than what they need any way. They were always proud to belong to families who were large slave owners, proud of the family name, and they did not like to belong to a man who owned but few slaves and they had a contempt for what they called "poor buckra" or "poor white folks." One who belonged to a man once who owned only him while at work said one day "d-m a man with one nigger." The poor and ignorant classes of whites do not like them either, so there is no "love lost" between them. I owned a negro once who met a white man in the road, both were driving ox teams. The negro would not give him room to pass but tried to run over him. The man came to me and I let him chastise the negro. The negro said when the man had whipped him with a switch "that poor white folks did not like him because he wore better clothes that they did." The white man got angry and whipped him again. It did no good.

I have never chastised but one of my negroes. He was my hog man looking after those that were in the river swamp on my place on the Bigbee River. He killed my hogs and sold the meat to the hands at the "Salt works" near by during the war for about half the value of the meat. He had plenty meat which he kept in a hole made under his house for the purpose. I think he deserved the punishment.

Booker Washington gives the negro good advice when he tells them to practice habits of economy, industry, and honesty or purpose. Strive to be respectable citizens by the accumulation of property and they will be successful and happy. There is no race problem to settle here for like "water it will seek its own level" and when Noah put his curse on Ham he placed his descendants the negro on his proper level. He is fit only for a servant for his brethren or fellow man. Mr. Cleveland in his speech with Booker Washington said the negro should not be the "hewers of wood and the drawers of water" always, but should have institutions of industrial training established for him. He had better have such institutions for them at the north and send for them if they are too good to do what they were created for, manual labor, and let the white man take hold as many of them do who are not able to live without labor in this country since the war.

The negro race will gradually pass away or "play out" in this country for since their day of emancipation many of them have become idle and worthless filling up jails, chain gangs, and penitentiaries and if they are not taken back to Africa from whence they came their places will be supplemented by industrious, thrifty white labor, and the race will become extinct in the United States.

The Darwin theory of evolution in the monkey family will be but a theory in fact for the monkey will not "evolute" and if a man is an ape he will be one on his "own hook" and the monkey will not be a man. Since the end of our civil war there has been a complete social revolution in the south and old time southern hospitality is a thing of the past.

We have often heard the remark that the "bottom rail is on top" since the war which means that many persons who owned no property before the war have made fortunes in some instances mostly on what the old original property owners have lost. It may be so in Cuba and South Africa and all countries suffering from the devastation of war but it is more especially so in our southern states since the war ended here.

In the south property has changed owners and passed into other hands. The old land marks are passing away and many families have surrendered their estates into the hands of syndicates and mortgages for money advanced to them as helpless farmers to make crops with the uncertainty of free negro labor to keep the "wolf from the door." Many men who never owned a negro before the war have made property by free negro labor on farms and own plantations by foreclosure of mortgages that never could have had the opportunity to get hold of such property before the war when the labor also was owned by the original land owners. Some have accumulated by charging big interest and commissions for money advanced to farmers. Every man in nine cases out of ten who can raise a little money builds himself a store and thinks he is a born merchant "cut out" for the business and while some succeed others who are "cut out" for the job find themselves "spoilt in the making and make money" over the left.

Speaking of the race problem the difference between the races here is that in color one white the other black and the only thing white about the black darky is the inside of his hands and feet for when they painted him he stood on his all fours and rather than discriminate against him on account of race color or previous condition they left him "status quo."

Aunt Penny was Uncle Ned's second wife. He had a wife when a young man in North Carolina who died there. Aunt Penny always cooked for the "overseer" at the plantation, milked the cows, and took care of the negro children left in the yard of the "overseer house." She sometimes would milk twenty five cows assisted by the youngsters to mind off the calves. I have often gone down there when a boy to get her nice corn bread, butter, and milk at the plantation. She made such nice corn bread and buttermilk I thought it better than that at home. The picture represents the "little negroes" at the "overseer house" when my mother would send her molasses for them to eat sitting around large tin pans filled with it. They would eat and smear it all over their mouths, faces, and hands while eating to their heart's content. My father would give his negroes a barbecue when the crop was laid by about the fourth of July. They enjoyed it very much by marching like masons about the place with dead grass fastened on a stick or pole to show they had conquered and killed the grass out of the corn and cotton.

Roden one of Aunt Dolls sons took charge of the masons, speaking French to them he had learned in Louisiana. He gave commands to his comrades in a language they thought was French but did not understand a word of it but would try to obey him. My father gave them whiskey to make them lively. They sang songs and made speeches in regard to killing the grass and putting the crop out of danger. Isaac Nordlinger, a young friend (merchant) from Suggsville, was present and enjoyed the fun very much.

Aunt Doll was an old family servant who came with my father and was his nurse when a child in North Carolina. She was never required to do any work except to nurse children. My father would not allow her to work. She not only served as his nurse but nursed all his youngest children born to my mother at home in Alabama; boys and girls. She always had her meals on a table to herself at home after the white family had finished and I can remember how she would ask "the blessing" in a whisper to herself before eating. She had several sons and daughters; three sons, Cambridge, Roden, and Isaac. Cambridge was my father's hostler and carriage driver nearly all his life and was carriage driver for my mother until after the war closed. We all looked upon "Aunt Doll" as one of the family. She was a privileged character about home but always behaved well and the children all loved her and she was fond of children. Old Mammy Lot was my mother's nurse and Mammy servant. She was mother of all her negro children and grandchildren inherited by her father's estate in South Carolina. She had several sons and daughters.

Frank and Bedford two of her sons drove the wagons in hauling. Frank was leader of the plow hands in "antebellum" days. Elbert was another son (blacksmith) and Dink was the carriage driver and carpenter. Mammy Lot lived in Mobile most of her time with her daughter, Louisa, who was emancipated with her children by a man who purchased her from my mother for that purpose. Mammy Lot was as free as she wished to be during her lifetime although she was a slave and had not been emancipated but belonged to my mother; as well as all of her descendants, children, and grandchildren who were many in numbers.

She came up from Mobile in summer or whenever she wished to visit my mother and her children who were at home or on the plantation. She always had her trunks full of goods and little things as presents for her children. She always called my mother "Levia" or Miss Puggy (nickname) her middle name being Olivia. Mammy Lot, Aunt Doll, and Aunt Penny (Uncle Ned's wife) all died after my father a good while before our civil war between the states. Mammy Lot lived longer and died I think after the other two had passed away. They have gone to "that bourne from whence no traveler returns."

May God bless the good old faithful servants in a world of eternal happiness and bless. God save the memory of the old time negro. The last one of whom will soon pass into the unknown to join the army of masters who have gone before and who await the coming of the faithful servant with arms open. We shall see their likes never again. We have passed the day of the good old black mammy whom we could go to with our troubles and be sure of words of comfort to our youthful souls; Meridian Star.

Earl of "Bassett's Creek" - Sir Wm Pritchett

"UNCLE WILL."

(134.)

Chapter V
The Good Life

My first school days or the first school I attended was a school for girls, taught by Dr. Pilate and his wife at Suggsville. Dr. Pilate was a Frenchman and his wife was an English lady. My father had a nice school house built with rooms for boarders and a large room for the school. Dr. Pilate was an accomplished Frenchman. He taught music, drawing, painting, and was a naturalist who could prepare birds by stuffing them after being killed for that purpose and he would put them in glass vases when finished which made them appear as if alive. He would also catch butterflies in nets, insects, snakes, and bugs and prepare them for inspection appearing to be alive after being prepared. Mrs. Pilate taught the school with other ladies to assist her in teaching. I was the only boy in school except her little boy named, Louis Philipe, for one of the royalty of France. I was in bad health and was too young to go by myself, although my oldest sister attended school. My mother sent a little negro girl to school with me for company to play together out of doors. I had only two lessons to recite in the morning and afternoon. My negro girl was called little Eliza as Mrs. Pilate had a hired woman named Eliza also.

When we had finished our lessons every day, Louis Pilate would come in the school room and say; "Mamma can Milton, and little Eliza, and I go out and play?"

She would say yes, and then we would often play the balance of the day.

Dr. Pilate and wife were accomplished teachers and they had a fine female school of young ladies. I went to school for my health, being very young. Dr. Pilate moved to Louisiana and the school was then taught by Miss Chandler from Mobile. We always called it the Pilate place. After the school closed my father planted mulberry trees there called Morus multicaulis mulberry, the leaves of which were food for the "silk worm" to feed upon to make silk. I do not remember how he succeeded in the venture as I was quite young. My brother Dr. B. S. Barnes lives on the same place where he built a residence after the war.

I was born as a matter of course or I would not have been here and although I was on hand and present at the time of my arrival in the terrestrial hemisphere I do not remember the day and date of that important event to me, but the old family record tells me that it was on the second day of March AD 1832 at my old home near Suggsville Clark County

Alabama. The reader will readily perceive upon this announcement that I have been on hand long enough to have often heard it "thunder" and that I am no "spring chicken" either. As I have mentioned before my father was from Scotland Neck Halifax County, North Carolina and his name was Samuel T. Barnes. He died at our home December fourteenth, 1848 at the age of fifty-three years leaving my mother with nine children all minors except the two eldest. I have no bible record with me as to the date of his birth but it was in the year 1795, if my memory serves me right. His mother was Rebecca Bryan and my name is Milton Bryan Barnes after her family. After the death of her first husband, my grandfather, which occurred when my father was only six weeks old and being the only child, they inherited my grandfather's fortune which I am told was quite large. My grandmother afterwards married Peyton Tunstall with whom she had several children; sons and daughters. My father had a half brother whose name was Payton Randolph Tunstall; nicknamed "flash" for his auburn hair. I called him "Uncle Flash" a handsome man. He had a fine black horse named, Ceola, after the Indian chief. Being named after the Randolph family, I presume the Tunstalls were related to them. I had a brother named Peyton Randolph Barnes who died quite young at our home near Suggsville.

I am a Presbyterian and believe whatever is to be will be if it never happens and if a man is born to be hanged you cannot kill him with a board axe, neither can you hang him if not so intended. Astrologists say that the stars and planets govern our fate and predict for me good luck for the future and that I will "come out of the kinks" after all.

So note it be, for there is a "Divinity that shapes our ends Rough hew them how you will." I am a Mason and have taken the Royal Arch Degree, an old soldier of the Lost cause and a democrat by birth, raised and educated in the Jeffersonian school not the kind that advocate sub-treasuries, government ownership of railroads and telegraph wires, which tends to centralize the power in the government.

These are measures which Jefferson fought against all of his life, and if he had lived till the present day, he would ask that party to drop his name. The Hamiltonian theory would have suited them better. "The government derives its power by the consent of the governed, and the Jeffersonian theory serves as a balance wheel to hold the machinery of the government together."

W. H. Harvey, Coin Harvey, so called in his book on "money trusts, and imperialism" says that if we do not dislodge the money power, meaning the Republican party, there is danger of our government drifting into a monarchy.

Eventually they will want a stronger government to keep the party in power, increase the regular army to large proportions and through the importation of ship loads of pauper soldiers from Europe, to force us into sub-mission in case of revolution by the people. God forbid such a calamity! They hold the reins of government and it seems a difficult matter to dislodge them unless the people rebel against trusts in the coming election, to overthrow the money power in control of the government. I do not wish to enter into any political discussion in my book and after a few words on political matters I am done. The democrats have been divided on the money question and we have not succeeded in the inauguration of but one President on the democratic ticket since the war, who caused a disruption of the party in his last administration himself "cow catcher behinds." The best friends (we have at the north are the "brave soldiers" who met us in hostile combat on the battle field and although they claim to be our friends and brothers now and the blue and the gray have shaken hands across the "bloody Chasm", and we are united people so called, they would not vote for a southern democrat for president to save his soul from perdition for defeat would be certain to the democratic party in case we should be so foolish as to nominate a southern man for the office on that ticket, neither do I believe they would vote a southern republican for president, as they have always had a bountiful supply of "Yankees" on hand to take charge of the job.

The woman prophetess of Paris whose predictions have come to pass published in the New York Journal to wit: among other events the assassination of Mr. McKinley says we are to have another terrible war with England in which we will be victorious after the loss by war of blood poured out from the veins of our best people. She says that the money power will be over thrown by the exasperation of the people and that Cuba Mexico, after the death of Diaz, all the South American Republics, and at last, Canada will be annexed to the United States. It would be a difficult matter to realize the existence of a government of such vast proportions and it would be a government of nations rather than states. Ambitious men would seek to control it and they would continue to create revolution in the Spanish American provinces which would require a tremendous standing army to keep it in subjection.

It would seem that such a government would crumble and fall by its own weight, the negro race problem would sink into oblivion forever, and we would be a strange conglomeration of nations, and a mongrel race indeed.

The first school for boys I attended was taught by G. W. Campbell in 1842 at Suggsville. He was a good old fashion teacher—would use the rod very often and taught in the old fashion style; made all our pens with a pen knife to write with in our copy books out of goose quills which were sold in all the stores at that time. The sessions were much longer and vacations shorter than at the present day so that children did not lose much time from school during the year. I attended several schools taught by different teachers afterwards at Suggsville. We were sometimes required by our teachers to read compositions and recite speeches on Friday afternoons preparing for what was called exhibitions at the end of the sessions. We enjoyed our exhibitions very much and the patrons and people in the surrounding country would attend.

At noon while attending school at Suggsville the boys would often in summertime run down to the mill pond, our "little mill", on the branch not very far off to swim and bathe in the pond. One day my brother Alfred got out of his depth in a deep place in the mill pond and if I had not called out very loud to the other boys to save him he would have drowned; he was strangling in a deep hole of water. When we were late getting back to school we returned in a hurry for fear our teacher would punish us for being late. One day I told one of the boys if he would jump in the pond of water with his clothes on I would give him five cents I had in my pocket. He wore cotton made pants at the time and holding out his hand he said, "give it here" and jumped off the dam before he had time to take the coin. He was of course as wet as a "drowned rat" but I gave him the half dime for his trouble. Brother Alfred and I at one time went to school in "Grove Hill" to Mr. Kilpatrick, and boarded at Woodlands hotel. I have never been punished at school in my life except one day by an Irishman named McGrot at Suggsville. He whipped me because I was not looking at my book at the time. He was one of the kinds that if you took him out of a book, he did not have sense enough to "get out of a shower of rain." He was an educated fool, fresh from Ireland. My father sent him his money with a message that if he spoke to him he would whip him, and took three children from his school. After I had finished school in Clark County, my oldest brother Dr. J. P. Barnes married his wife at Claiborne, Monroe County on the Alabama river; Miss Amelia Allen whose father a merchant of the firm of Smith and Allen died in Claiborne Alabama. I boarded with Mr. Smith and wife while at school there. They were strict old fashion Presbyterians which gave me a predilection for said church by attending church and Sunday school when a boy. I joined the Presbyterian Church at Talladega Alabama under Dr. Otts of Greensboro after becoming a man of middle age not having the opportunity before that time.

Prof. A. B. Goodhue was my first teacher at Claiborne. He went to Marion Alabama from there. Bliss was my next teacher there and both northern men - going to "Bliss" ought to have made me happy at any rate. Barclay took a class also in his office of private pupils—he was a lawyer at that time practicing his profession at Claiborne. I was at Claiborne in 1846 when the Mexican war was going on and I often went to see the soldiers going down in the steamboats on the river bound for Mexico. The picture of the steamer, Sunny South, drawn by me, is a specimen of the side wheel steamer in those days on the Alabama River. I remember the Sunny South came down the river one day.

The river was very high and Sandy Rone, an old Clark County friend was pilot at the wheel. As she came floating down below the landing very fast he shut off steam and going ahead on one wheel swung her around completely and landed without any trouble. I thought it was the most magnificent management of a steamboat I had ever seen.

Sandy Rone survived his wife in Clark County and afterwards was a planter on the river above Gainestown. He was a man of great wit and humor and had many friends. He tried steam boating again after the war but his health failed, and he died at home where I helped to put him in his last earthly resting place.

The first girl claimed by me as a sweetheart was while a school boy at Claiborne. She was the daughter of a lawyer who lived in Claiborne. I was only about fifteen years old and thought that if I did not marry her that my chances for matrimony were ruined forever. Her father moved to an upper-county up the river. She soon got married after finishing her education. It was only a light case of school boy love but like all things mortal and evanescent it is only a thing of the past and she had, "Gone glimmering through the days that were—like a school boy's tale—the wonder of the hour."

After finishing school at Claiborne my father had always said he intended me to be a book keeper and "Uncle Eddy" Smith of the late firm Smith and Allen sold out to Abney and Dishman and took me in the counting room with him to learn book keeping. I had boarded with him a long while and he and wife, having no children, treated me like their own son at their house. Mrs. Smith was particularly nice about everything at home. Being a strict old fashion Presbyterian, she believed in predestination or foreordination to the letter and that whatever took place in our lives was so intended from the beginning of our existence here. For instance if two persons were married it was their lot to be joined together by divine power from date of birth. She thought that, "Whom the Lord hath joined together, let no man put asunder." I say so too and I am incline to think that all happy marriages are providential and are made through the instrumentality of our Creator and it is said that marriages are made up in Heaven, but it seems that some persons are unfortunate in their matrimonial alliances and badly mismatched. Josh Billings said "You frequently see a bay and a sorrel together" and if the "Old Boy" does not have a hand in the matchmaking they "kick up the devil" sometimes between themselves anyhow.

Mrs. Smith my old friend was so good and kind to me that I shall always feel a fond remembrance of her in the long! Long ago, while my life shall last for as I have said before, she had everything particularly nice for me—put pound cake in my tin bucket very often for me to take to school, and my mother used to tell me that the old lady had spoilt me with her extreme care and kindness while staying there.

One day while at home, I went into the kitchen where our old cook was baking cakes and asked her for one.

She said "Go way Mars Milton, I thought Mrs. Smith done astonished you wid cake."

She meant the old lady had spoilt me by giving me so much cake that I would not eat it.

Claiborne at that time was a prosperous town—all the cotton from Conecuh and Monroe Counties was hauled to that point and a good deal of business was done there on that account, but after a while they built a railroad from Montgomery to Mobile which cut off all the cotton that had been hauled and shipped to Mobile from there. It has been a dead town ever since.

Purdue Hill a nice little village settlement about two miles out from the river has taken its place. Claiborne after being deserted had no stores left except a little Jew store or two, like Goldsmith, who dealt in cowhides and "bis vax" as he called it.

Some one went there one day and said to him, "Goldsmith you got a store yet?"

He said yes! "spiter h-l if I don't sell on more gudes yesterday den I did tomorrow I will go down in to de vudes and pite myself mit a snake."

His oldest boy named Julius, who was a great help to him in his store, died which grieved him very much.

He said he didn't know, "vot dey vant to kill dat boy for—he vas a gude boy—he never done any poddy any ding—I vude rudder de pest cow I had shall tie den fur dat boy to tie."

At onetime the town was so full of Jews that they had almost full possession of it.

Bill Dabney a man of desperate character at Claiborne while on a "spree" one day took it into his head to exterminate the Jews in town or to run them all away. He first commenced by cutting a large piece from their oats as he met them on the street with a "bowie knife." He made an attempt to kill one named "Strider" in Levi and Jacobson's store but was prevented from doing so by two men pulling him off the man while trying to cut his throat. He then took down a new gun from the store and going over to another store across the street kept by an American named Felker asked for ammunition saying that he was going "dutch hunting." Felker told him to take as much ammunition as he wanted and to kill every Jew in town. I was standing in the door of our store when a Jew came running up the street with Dabney following him. The little Jew ran into our store and I told him to go into the back room until Dabney had passed the door. The Jew ran across the backyard and jumping over the fence went in a hurry towards the warehouse on the river where Dabney met him— killing him instantly by filling him with buck shot from head to foot.

We all went around to where we heard the gun fire, and Dabney came back and upon meeting Dr. Moore said, "Go around and see what you can do for him doctor for I threw him like an old buck."

It was Israel Jacobson lying on a bale of cotton killed by a new gun taken from his brother's store by a man with whom he was not acquainted.

The poor fellow was a very young man and had not been here long from Europe and could not speak English. Dabney being a man of such desperate character utterly reckless of the destruction of human life, no officer was willing to risk his own life by making an attempt to arrest him, in fact I learned that the magistrate was afraid to issue a warrant for his arrest, and as he had killed only a little friendless Jew whom in those days were not considered people of much consequence or respectability, he made his escape and fled to Texas. While there he changed his name to Winston which was his middle name, and was located at Richmond, Fort Bend County, Texas. It seems he was still reckless. He met his match however with a man of the same caliber who carved him up with a "bowie knife," which in that country was at that time a part of a man's everyday apparel. He was so badly used up that after the fight ended he exclaimed, " I am a dead man."

He afterwards recovered from his wounds and got well, but in another difficulty killed a man in a saloon at Richmand Texas because the man asked him to drink. He told the man he did not wish to drink.

The man insisted repeatedly and he finally said to him that if he did not let him alone he would hurt him. The man made fun of the remark and Dabney plunged his knife into him killing him instantly. He went to Houston from Richmand and stopped at the Old Capitol hotel.

The sheriff of Fort Bend County summoned a posse of men, and going to Houston found him in his room locked up. They broke the door in and Dabney was found sitting up in his bed with a pistol in each hand. He saw in an instant that the "game was up" with him and that death was his portion if he resisted "he threw up the sponge," and was a prisoner at last. Jackson at Claiborne Alabama, whose brother he had killed made a requisition for him to be brought to Alabama, and going to Texas brought him to Monroeville and lodged him in jail there. He was taken to Mobile jail for safe keeping where he remained sometime. To show the reckless character of the man, he told some one that in coming across the Gulf he tried to get an opportunity, being allowed to walk around with an officer, to throw Jacobson a brother of the man he killed, overboard and drown him in which case he was willing to drown himself by going over into the Gulf with him. He was a man of great magnanimity of character, at the same time he was no doubt an unhappy man from some cause and he said his life was no pleasure to him acknowledging that he had been crossed in his with love matters.

He could be depended upon where he pledged his word. One of his lawyers said while in the Mobile jail, the jailer would allow him to visit his office alone and return to jail when he had consulted him. At one time, the prisoners broke jail, no one was there except the jailor's wife at the time Dabney, a prisoner himself, called for a gun which the woman soon brought, and he told them to walk back into the jail everyone of them or he would shoot into them. They very quickly walked back, himself among them, to be locked up again. His trial came off in Monroeville. I was cited to appear as a witness against him. I was in the store when the Jew man ran in. I had to attend the trial about the time a friend of mine was married at Gainestown, Dr. LL Alston of Grove Hill. He wished me to be his best man—I could not be with him on that momentous occasion.

Dabney had able lawyers to defend him, Governor Bagby and Percy Walker of Mobile. D. C. Anderson of Mobile was solicitor and prosecuting attorney for the state. He was convicted of murder in the first degree with a life sentence in the penitentiary. Felker, the merchant who gave him ammunition to kill the Jews, disappeared for parts unknown. It is a singular coincidence that Dr. Alston, who wished me to be with him at his wedding, was one of the posse from Richmond Texas who arrested Dabney, being in Texas at that time practicing medicine.

Dabney remained in prison till the war began. He had a sister in New Orleans who worked faithfully for his release and the governor pardoned him on a petition from his friends signed by the jury who tried him in court at Monroeville. I saw him in Montgomery during the war working in a warehouse. He said that the testimony of Dr. Moore and myself convicted him. He did not blame me and introduced me as his friend. He said he had quit fighting and would not take part in a difficulty unless he was assaulted or in a case of self defense. He said he did not doubt the fact of his having killed the Jew but said he had no remembrance of it. He had been on a drinking, gambling "spree" for several days and most likely was in an insane condition of mind, "delirium tremens" perhaps. He walked erect and did not appear to be drunk that day, but acted in a very reckless manner. He was a fine type of physical manhood—such is the result of reckless folly and dissipation. I presume he never married. He was last seen on a steamboat bound for Mobile on the Alabama River since the war, and his destination no one knows now.

After my father died in the year 1848, I remained but a short time at Claiborne in a store there and having a disagreement with one of the firm of Abney and Dishman, I returned to my home at Suggsville Alabama. My father made a codicil to his will before his death bequeathing to me besides my share of his estate his riding pony "Cricket", his gun, and watch. I have the gun and watch yet and a picture of my pony "Cricket" which is about all I have left of his estate having been unfortunate in some of my business matters since the war. I have spoken of "Cricket" before. He was a handsome clay-bank with black mane and tail and died at the plantation.

I next went to Selma to attend school in 1849-1850 at the Masonic institute under Professor Wright and lady, male and female department. The old court house at Selma was built for the female institute by Masonic fraternity. I cannot recall anything especially important that happened to me while there, only that it was two sessions of my school days which was a very pleasant and happy period of my life. It is common to boys of any age at that time.

Chapter VI
Sweet Sixteen

I always claimed a sweetheart and sometimes more than one. There was one who seemed to take a special fancy to me, which can not be accounted for, unless she was at the age of romance —"Sweet sixteen" or there about. That is the romantic time in a girl's age. She thought she could not go through this world without me—as world of trials and vicissitudes as well as a world of happiness and bliss. Time rolled on and at the end of the school session I went home of course like all school boys do, for the reason they have no where else to go. My sweetheart went to the Johnson school. I had not suffered from love enough to lose any sleep at night on that account, and the truth is I did not know what the "tender passion" meant only a touch of it at Claiborne, and by the way, I like to have forgotten the fact that, the Claiborne girl was a pupil in the Masonic female department herself. So I had two—one in each school, Johnson's and the Masonic institute and was not in love enough to hunt either. The one at the Johnson and myself were engaged anyhow. We exchanged rings. It soon wore off with me for "absence conquers love" in a light case of the disease, like I had then, for very young people like me do not suffer much in contagious ailments anyway. We did not correspond long after my return home before the engagement was broken. I wrote to her that I had not finished my education and thought it best for us to quit. She answered by abusing me for my heartless conduct and sent me back my ring saying that if I had not thrown hers away I could keep it. I felt so mean about it that I gave it maybe to a friend. Years later while traveling I met her again. She looked at me although not a young man of nineteen, but an old man with white hair and beard. She recognized me in an instant and called my name. She had thought of me she said often but thought I was dead long ago. She lived in a house which appeared like herself as if it had seen its best days. I felt sorry for her for I was in trouble myself; poor suffering humanity! When we have thrown off this "mortal coil" what next? Shall it be eternal happiness or fearful punishment when grim death claims its own?

"Oh! A wonderful stream is the river of Time
As it runs through realms of tears
With a faultless rhythm and a musical rhyme
And a broader sweep and a surge sublime

That blends with the ocean of years.
How the winters are drifting like flakes of snow
And the summer like buds between
And the year in the sheaf so they come and go
On the rivers breast with its ebb and flow
As it glides in the shadow and sheen.
There is a magical isle up the river Time
When the softest of airs are playing.
There's a cloudless sky and a tropical clime
And a song as sweet as a vesper chime
And the Junes with the roses are staying.
And the name of the isle is the long ago
And we bury our treasures there.
There are bows or beauty and bosoms or snow.
There are heaps of dust but we love them so.
There are trinkets and tresses of hair.
There are fragments of song that nobody sings
And part of an infant's prayer.
There's a lute unswept and a harp without strings.
There are broken vows and pieces of rings
And the garments she used to wear.
There are hands that are waved when the fairy shore
By the mirage is lifted in air
And we sometimes hear through the turbulent roar
When the wind down the river is fair.
Oh! Remember for aye be the blessed isle.
All the day of life till night.
When the evening comes with its beautiful smile
And our eyes are closing to slumber awhile.
May that greenwood of Soul be in sight.

When I returned home from Selma school, my notion was to carry out my father's plan to enter into a mercantile life and had concluded to go into a commission house in Mobile with a gentleman who had been my father's commission merchant for a long while. He had promised to take me in with him before my father died.

In the meantime a young man a good friend of mine at Suggsville persuaded me to take up the study of medicine with him as he was about to commence under the instruction of his uncle, a physician there. We read together in a private office for about twelve months and were ready to attend medical lectures at New Orleans. He went to New Orleans and my oldest brother, a physician in Mobile, knowing my age, said I had better stay with him and read longer in his office in Mobile; that I was very young and had plenty time anyway my father's estate was not settled and having no other means to go with I remained in Mobile in his office to continue the study of medicine. I found it a difficult matter to read in an office on first floor of Royal Street where it seemed someone was constantly coming in to talk and interrupt me. I did better up the country in a quiet room with no one to disturb me. One day after being out on the street a while I walked in and found a gentleman talking to cousin Milton and my brother, who he introduced as a relative of ours. I had heard my brother speak of him often, and found him very clever and friendly.

When he left the office he said to me, "when you go home you "take up" your grip sack and get on a steam…"

Cousin Milton went out and in a few minutes bought her father and myself a "toddy" with nutmeg on it. She showed me which was mine and in a modest way I drank it. I did not "indulge much" about that time, but have "made it squat" since, but not in late years. My life has been a strange one. I stayed with them about a week and in the meantime went to a wedding at Eutaw Alabama the county site of Greene.

At that time General McQueen married Miss Pickens one of the "belles" of the town. We returned to the family mansion called, Rosemount, which was a splendid building, a wealthy southern planter's home. I enjoyed myself so much while there that I took my leave with regret, and in attending the wedding, felt that my relatives, and especially my "pretty cousin," had done me a great kindness in introducing me into the society of such nice people at the wedding among the "elite" of Eutaw.

Before leaving Rosemount my "cousin" promised to correspond with me if I would write first. I wrote from Mobile and received an answer in due time then came the "tug of war" it was the commencement of a period of my existence which changed the whole course of my future life. She came down on a visit to Mobile to a lady relative, and while there I called on her, and one night we went to the theater, I well remember, to see the performance by the "great wizard" of the north so called slight of hand and legerdemain. I enjoyed her society very much while there but in the mean time my brother-in-law, Robert Harwell, who married my oldest sister and moved to Louisiana came over and on his return insisted on my going home with him to see my sister, his wife. I hated to leave about that particular time, my "pretty cousin" in Mobile, but yielding to the persuasion of my brother-in-law I went to Louisiana on a visit to my sister.

He lived on bayon Teche St Landry parish not far from Opelousas. He had a pretty little plantation on the bayou and engaged in planting for sugar. His house was very nice and comfortable, and the country was beautiful to behold. I have always thought that the country in St Landry Parish was the most lovely and beautiful I have ever seen in my life in the section in which Opelousas is located.

In passing through New Orleans I bought a copy of "Uncle Tom's Cabin" just out by Mrs. Harriet Beecher Stowe, sister to Henry Ward

Beecher the great abolition preacher of Brooklyn, New York; the man who went to England during our war and took active part in exerting himself to prevent the recognition of our Confederacy by that country. I do not know whether my book "Uncle Ned's cabin" should be called a counterpart of an off set to "Uncle Tom's Cabin," but I do know that my book is true to the letter "verbatim et literatim" of incidents to which I can testify myself. Before leaving Louisiana my brother-in-law sold me a pair of white ponies with a light buggy to which I drove them. They were of a light cream color and had light blue eyes. They were you might say complete "blondes" in color and complexion. One of them was a good riding pony and as the "hair-lip man" would say you could "yute on him" all day. He was my hunting pony when driving for deer in the "pine woods" as the picture of the "deer hunt" represents. I have killed a good many deer while hunting on him. Harwell Goodwin in the picture hunted on his pony Old Blaze. Jimmy Mobley, Harwell Goodwin and myself were boon companions who often went over the creek in the pine woods hunting for deer. Old "Uncle Will" the "Earle of Bassett's Creek" so called by my uncle Dr. Tunstall, my fathers half brother, was an old negro who belonged to Mrs. Pritchett at Suggsville and although a slave, was free in fact, and did as he pleased in staying with wife and children to take care of the old Pritchett place near "Bassett's Creek." He was fond of hunting and went often with us driving for deer on his mare but he never killed any of them that I can remember.

BiLL Murphy, Blacksmith

Barlow Bend.

Chapter VII
Camp Scene

I was always what was called a "good shot" in hunting deer and when I "pulled down" on an old buck with my gun, he was mine. Three of us went down once to Walker Springs on "Bassett's Creek" taking a one mule wagon and an old darkie named Peter along. It was in October and camping in the creek swamp gave me a chill the first night caused by malaria which will happen sometimes. I was riding "Old Cricket" my clay bank pony and went home next day with a hot-fever. I could hardly sit upon him and was in a delirious condition when I got home. I could not tell my mother what was the matter. I tried to tell her, but would forget what to say. She put me in my bed upstairs, but soon had me taken to a room joining hers downstairs. She sent for Dr. Files and I did not know anything in five days and nights, not even when they brought me down stairs. One night while they were all standing around my bedside expecting me to die about nine o'clock my eyes opened all at once, and I asked them what was the matter? They told me I was very sick. I recovered very rapidly from that time on and soon got well.

Soon after I recovered from my spell of sickness they had a Methodist "camp meeting" at Suggsville near the "Indian Spring" very close to our house. My mother being a pillar of the church had a tent and calling upon "Uncle Ned" again, soon had one erected to suit her. She even had a parlor fixed up for her lady friends with a nice fireplace and chimney and also a carpet put on the floor. One of the young men who was along when I was taken sick at the camp hunt who was a wicked sort of a fellow was converted at the "camp meeting" and he went immediately into the pulpit taking a vow on himself to forever forsake his sins and became a preacher for the balance of his life which was a surprise to his friends, knowing him to be so wild before. His father being a Methodist preacher might have caused him to reform.

I wrote to "my cousin" about the "camp meeting" and told her of the young ladies who were there in great numbers, but there was none there like her and that I had rather be with her than all of them put together. It pleased her.

Chapter VIII
Bill Murphy

The picture which represents Bill Murphy the colored blacksmith of Barlow Bend, Clark County was a unique character. Bill was a hard working, old darkie in his shop. He made an honest living and was a good-hearted old soul. He was fond of his dram and it is said the "three scruples make a drachma," but Bill took his dram without any scruples at all. He was happy when on his mustang pony with a bottle of the "Queen's eye water" in his pocket and would say when full of whiskey and a heart full of the milk of human kindness to his fellow man."

I am a good old negro.

He was only the worst enemy to himself like the most of drinking men black and white. He had the misfortune to have a stiff leg in the knee joint which made him look quite game on his mustang pony.

He would brace himself up and bare down on that leg. I met him one day and said to him, "Bill rise and shine and show your game leg."

He said, "I is Mr. Barnes!"

Bill and his father were slaves of ex-governor Murphy of Alabama; one of the first state executives. Bill had a son, among others, kidnapped or induced to go aboard a ship for employment at Mobile; carried to Cuba and sold as slaves after being emancipated here. Bill lived several years after the war and died at home near Barlow Bend.

Chapter IX
Love

Tis said that, "the course of true love never runs smooth." Not always so, but in many instances it is "Oh! Woman in our hours of ease, uncertain, coy, and hard to please. But when sickness and sorrow afflict the brow, a ministering angel thou, is something I do not quite remember, but words quoted from Byron.

I know one thing a smart woman is often hard to understand. They will say no when they mean yes and "kick" a fellow hard when they like him as hard as they kick. "My cousin" was not only beautiful, but elegant in manner and bearing. She had many offers of marriage and was considered a "belle," not a fashionable belle, but on her own merit. She had a good deal of plain "common sense" and her family were practical people. She was never the less very ambitious and placed her ideal high. I think that women of great ambition of ten strike high, but do not find their ideal in marriage every time for by having many offers they become indifferent and hard to please. They refuse many until they come to the "jumping off place," then it may be anybody, Lord, to keep from being an old maid.

We kept up our correspondence and I finally went to Rosemount again. It seemed to me that it had an attraction for me that no other place had ever had. They were always kind and hospitable, but as I said "true love does not run smooth." I came away with a "flea in my ear." Our correspondence was kept up continually for three years. I finally wrote her a long loving letter expressing my great admiration and deep attachment for her with the hope of its being reciprocated in return. She answered by saying that she was surprised that she had written me as an affectionate cousin "a place she wished to retain in regard to me and although my letter had been repeatedly read she could not be convinced as to the reality of its purport." She hoped that time and absence would change my feelings and she would always hold me in fond remembrance as one of her "best friends." As old "Uncle Ned's'" favorite tune said my "cakes were all dough."

She wrote me that her brother was to be married soon and gave me a cordial invitation to come. I went and acted as his best man with a young lady of her neighborhood. It is a strange thing what trifling incidents may do to change a man in such matters. I rode with her in a carriage to the wedding and another married lady also rode in the same vehicle with us.

In coming back, the young lady with whom I waited got in the carriage and "my cousin" remarked to me after I had been seated that I had better ride in a carriage behind as it might be to heavy on the horses going home. I got out of course and immediately another young man took my place in the carriage. How would you kind reader have liked it? After we reached her home, the wedding party went to the river going to Mobile. I rode in the carriage behind and took my valise along going home on the boat. She heard me say I was going and seemed to hate it about my riding behind in a carriage after going with her to the wedding.

I went down to the river dissatisfied and gloomy. Our correspondence continued. In one of her letters she sent me a "blue violet." I acknowledged its reception by a quotation which said: "Oh! Only those whose souls have felt; this one idolatry can tell how precious the slightest thing is; which affection gives and hallows. A dead flower will long be kept remembrances of looks that made each leaf a treasure." She wrote me once that she intended to visit a relative in Mobile soon and in reply we made arrangements to meet there.

I went to Mobile and called on her at a gentleman's house. She was glad to see me. There was another young lady came with her and next day I took a friend with me to call on them. That night we went all hands to a minstrel show. I let my friend go with her that night, but afterwards met her at the theater and talked with her a while. I called to see her next day to bid her good bye. I was not satisfied with my visit and wrote to her of my hopeless condition for I could not talk to her about it, but could tell it all in writing. She answered and said she regretted my unfortunate attachment for her and gave me no encouragement.

I confess that I could not understand her and was completely "hacked" for "faint heart never won fair lady" yet perhaps that was it. I was young and inexperienced in such things and did not know what to do. My father's half brother, my uncle Dr. Tunstall, had come to see us from Texas having lost his wife there but on his return asked me to go with him. I went to Texas and meeting her brothers in Mobile one of them said his sister had given him a letter to mail to me before leaving home, but he had forgotten it. I did not receive it; such neglect ruins us often forever.

Chapter X
Texas

I went to Texas and stayed about three months there. It was cold winter but I had a good time and saw a great deal of fine country while there. I saw a good many deer and went hunting too. When I returned home in the spring I met the young lady's brother in Mobile who informed me of his sisters approaching marriage soon to a gentleman from Mississippi and invited me to come. I did not go. I never saw the gentleman but heard that he was a wealthy cotton planter, a widower with children. The fragrant rose was not for me and "Whom the Lord hath joined together, Let no man put asunder."

I heard that they had been unfortunate and lost all by the war. He was afterwards appointed as consul to Cuba, but unfortunately took yellow fever and died at Trinidad. I heard that my "cousin" after being left a widow with a large family on her hands died at her home in Mississippi. I hope she has gone to that house not made with hands eternal in the Heavens. Her father gave up Rosemount "this fine plantation to his youngest son who married the daughter of Alcorn. He had 500 bales of cotton bound for Liverpool captured on the sea by "Yankee pirates" since our "lost cause." He died after the war. One of his sons was a member of our last State Legislature of Alabama. Peace to the memory of my "beautiful cousin" the elegant "belle of Rosemount."

Chapter XI
Bigbee River Farm

After leaving my brother's office in Mobile, I abandoned the ideal of pursuing the study of medicine and having disposed of my interest in the old plantation to my mother, I bought a place on the Bigbee river below Jackson near the central "Salt works" in which Salt creek ran through and emptied into the river at my landing. I bought the place from R. P. Carney who once owned Carney's bluff just below. He was an old bachelor and moved to Ohio to emancipate some negroes which would have been done by remaining here anyway if he could have foreseen the results of our coming war. He was a singular sort of a man and being noted for his drollery and humor his friends sometime would go to see him to hear him talk.

I once spent a day at his house with two other friends and he told some anecdotes of incidents which happened while he was in the Florida war. He was orderly sergeant of his company and one night while the moon was shinning brightly the alarm was given that the Indians were coming to attack their camp. There was a man in the company Bill L one of his neighbors from Clark County who became very much excited about the Indians coming. Bill was what might be compared in description to the "vegetable gentleman" he had a "freckle face, redish whiskers, turn-up nose, carroty hair, and perhaps a squash foot." Bill and the Sergeant were near together both behind pine trees with their guns ready for the fray. The Sergeant said he was so excited he could not hold his gun steady.

All at once Bill became very thirsty for water and said to him "Sergeant Carney! I want a little wattar, if I had a little wattar, I could fight a little bettar." He said to Bill, "Hold on Bill! Mind your tree and I will mind mine."

He bawled out again "if I had some wattar I could fight a little bettar."

The sergeant went down the hill to a spring of water but had nothing with which to get it except a "frying pan" with a long handle. He dipped up the water with the "frying pan" on his shoulder went up the hill to find that the water had all spilt out behind on the ground before he got to Bill. He tried again with better success but in the confusion of noise looking for the Indians to come found it to be only "a drove of cattle on a stampede" which ran over them, false alarm.

Chapter XII
Traveling

Before settling down on my place on the Bigbee River I felt a desire to travel while I had an opportunity to see something of the world. My mother, sister and brother-in-law, (the latter being recently married), my youngest sister, and myself formed the traveling party and we first stopped at Nashville where my younger brother was at the military college under Bushrod Johnson. After the exercises were through at the Nashville College we went to Montvale Springs in Tennessee and found it a nice cool place at the foot of a tall mountain. We remained there about a week and stopping a while at White Sulfur Springs in Virginia. We continued our route to Washington City. While there we saw all the sights and visited the White House and Congress Hall at the Capitol being in the summer season, we found Washington very dry and dull. Congress was not in session. The President was absent, but we went into the Senate chamber and saw the names of our distinguished men on the back of their seats. We went down the Potomac river to Mount Vernon and saw the residence of General Washington and went into the rooms, the one in which General Washington died and had our pictures taken together in front of his burial place or tomb. My mother and party returned home from Washington and I went to New York through Baltimore and Philadelphia. I felt free from all encumbrances and made up my mind to take in all the sights which came to hand and I remained in New York about three weeks in all, visiting Saratora and Niagara Falls. Colonel Portis from Suggsville was with me and we saw Blondin walk a rope across Niagara River at an elevation of several hundred feet above the water dashing below to the Canada side while a band of music played on both sides of the river during the performance. It was fearful to behold the dangerous feat, but I thought I could stand it if he could.

In leaving New York for Saratoga and Niagara Falls I forgot to mention that we took a steamboat going up the Hudson River to Albany. The Hudson is a beautiful stream and we passed by West Point and the place where Van Buren lived; also saw many handsome country seats and residences where the wealthy people of New York spent their summers at that time. I presume that the millionaires of the present day, having accumulated such vast fortunes at the north find it too quiet and tame on the Hudson, but spend their time and money in Europe, this country not being large enough to hold them.

We found nothing very remarkable at Saratoga, except the fine hotels and nice accommodations there, besides the spring of congress water paved in the marble where a small boy was ready to hand you a dipper of congress water. We saw the place where they were bottling if by machinery for general use in all the Hotels everywhere. They even put the corks in that way, after filling the bottles giving them an income of $125,000 per annum for the sale of it. They always put a bucket of congress water in your room besides one of free stone fresh from the spring.

We then left for Niagara Falls. It is a great natural curiosity. The water tumbles over the falls making a roaring noise like an approaching storm; the volume of which is eighteen feet through on the verge of the falls in "Terripan tower" which I shall always remember having seen a most beautiful woman from Canada. She had an escort who appeared to be an Englishman from his dress and appearance. We went across the suspension bridge to Canada side where there was a hotel. The railroad ran over the top of the bridge while vehicles and pedestrians went through the bridge below. Colonel Portis, a lawyer from Suggsville, whom I have mentioned before, and myself returned to New York together and we soon left for Washington D.C. where we obtained a patent for a soldiers claim at the government land office for 160 acres of land belonging to my mother left to her as the only living heir to the uncle who died in soldiers hospital at Savannah Georgia in the War of 1812.

We left for home going by the way of Carthage, Illinois where the land had been located and sold for taxes. We saw the "old jail" where the Mormon prophet Smith and his followers were killed by a mob at Carthage when they were located there. The cars travel very fast in that country but they were just building a new road to Carthage and they moved so slow that I felt like "Artemus Ward" who told the conductor on a new road up there that he had better put his "cow catcher" on behind for fear the "cows might slip up and bite the passengers."

My mother had a chance to redeem her soldiers claim on the land sold for taxes at Carthage, but the war broke out and after it ended we found out by consulting a lawyer who happened to be Adlea E. Stevenson of Bloomington, Illinois, Vice President with Cleveland afterwards, whose name was given me by writing to Jno T. Morgan, that the land was lost and could not be redeemed under the statue of limitations. I will beg pardon of the reader for a mistake I have made in "getting ahead of the hounds" by going too fast in my previous chapter by arriving at Carthage, Illinois without mentioning our route through Ohio and Indiana first, for we went so fast that we traveled through both states in one day without stopping from Washington to Cincinnati and I do assure you that we did not need the "cow catcher behind to keep the cows from biting the passengers." We remained in Cincinnati one night after leaving Washington that day and then made our way to Carthage, Illinois where my mother's land was sold for taxes. Colonel Portis and myself struck out from Carthage by private conveyance towards Keokuk in Iowa lying on the Mississippi river and crossing the river in a canoe we found a steamboat bound for St. Louis. We did not go up into town not having time to do so, but were soon on our way down the river. Our boat did not go any farther down than St. Louis and we waited there until next day and found another steamer a very fine boat, Imperial, bound for New Orleans. We stopped at Cairo a place at the mouth of the Ohio River. That night they had a big fire at Cairo which nearly destroyed the town. While we were lying at Cairo, another boat, the Choctaw, came down. I was sick and had to take my birth on the Imperial. It so happened that we were acquainted with the clerk and a man from Memphis who had an interest in the Choctaw both old acquaintances of ours. Colonel Portis becoming impatient to get home quicker advised me to go down on the Choctaw to New Orleans as I was sick and knew the clerk, besides she would be off sooner than the Imperial. It was just the other way, the Imperial left first and beat us to New Orleans. She was much the finest and best craft of the two.

Chapter XIII
Races & Cities

I have neglected to mention anything that I saw in the city of New York not wishing to make a tedious job of my book but will merely mention that while I remained in the city I boarded at the St. Nicholas hotel three weeks and met with many friends every day from Alabama. Among them were two old school mates of the Masonic Institute; Phil Weaver of Selma, and Dave Myer from Montgomery. We hired a carriage one day and drove down twelve miles to see Flora Temple and Princess trot on the "Long Island" race track. Flora Temple won in two minutes and twenty-one seconds called the fast time then, but not so now in this fast age.

After a tedious trip with Captain Weibling on the steamer Choctaw coming down the Mississippi river in very hot summer weather from Cairo, we arrived at New Orleans. I continued my journey to Mobile and went to the "Battle House" which compared well for neatness and comfort with all first class hotels I had seen on my tour since leaving home. Mobile felt like home a quiet nice clean looking little city of my native state Alabama which means "here we rest." I did rest for I was sick and kept my room. While at the hotel in Mobile, I sent for a physician, but did not like to remain there under medical treatment long, but went up to Mauville on the M&O railroad to my brothers about twenty miles from the city for medical treatment under him, who was well known as a prominent physical in Mobile at the time, Dr. John P. Barnes. I recovered my health in about six weeks. While there I showed them some pictures of different views of Niagara Falls taken on glass which I obtained there. In showing them to visitors at my brother's, a lady one day accidentally knocked off the one representing "Blondin" walking across the river several hundred feet high in the air above the water dashing below and broke it into small pieces on the floor. She was very sorry, but it was gone. I returned to the city on my way home and while there stepped into a tobacco store to buy a box of cigars for my brother at Mauville and the man in the store being an agent for the Havana lottery in Cuba had on exhibition some lottery tickets in his show case. I asked the price of one which I purchased for five dollars. It drew me one-fourth of a whole ticket giving one hundred dollars taking off ten per cent discount for commission.

Chapter XIV
Home again!

I will say, home again, "all quiet on the Potomac" and will also beg of my readers that if parts of my narrative seem stale and uninteresting to them that it is a true statement of incidents in my past life important to me and not a romance to the young novel reader of either sex who delight in the fictional tale on stern reality "with the cow catcher behind" nor a book for them to sit up all night and cry over parts of which they know to be a lie. I have always filled the position of a man myself and if my book does not suit the "woman's Kingdom" it relates principally to me and I will only ask that you pass my imperfections by.

I had almost forgotten my match of Louisiana ponies which I brought home on my return from there on my former visit to my oldest sister living on bayon Teche near Opelous St. Laudry Parish which was, I have always thought to be the most beautiful country I have ever seen. My ponies were creams with light blue eyes and as I have said of them before might be called "blondes" one of them as seen in the picture was a nice hunting animal and the other was not much under the saddle. I soon got tired of them and traded them for a nice iron gray horse which I called blue skin. I got him from my old friend now Dr. Callier.

After coming to my mother's home at Suggsville, I remained there until fall or winter and moved down to my place, which I bought before taking my trip north and west, on the Bigbee which I called the "Dirt Dobber's nest." It was only a double log cabin with two rooms and an entry between which looked as near like the picture I have made with a pencil from memory of it over forty years ago as could be made with a photograph camera. It was the house Mr. Carney occupied when I bought it with the exception of the shelter I put in front. You will no doubt readily imagine the change of residence into such a lonely place after having traveled and stopped at first class hotels everywhere. Suffice it to say I had enough to eat such as people live on in the country and had no one to care for except myself, but still I was not happy for I have long since found out that there is no true happiness on earth and that the "island of contentment is not laid down on the map." My house did all for me that a palace could do, that is it was comfortable in hot weather and I had two fire places and plenty of fuel in winter. It kept off rain in wet weather and like the Arkansas traveler's house; it did not "leak a drop when it did not rain." It had stick and dirt chimneys dobbed with clay and the cracks of the house outside was also filled with clay to keep the cold out in winter and is the reason I called it "The Dirt Dobber's Nest" and I was the only occupant which made me the "dirt dobber" aforesaid.

I put my darkies to work on the place by commencing to clear more land and in the swamp for cultivation as there was not enough already cleared. The back water came up and overflowed it near the river which put me to the trouble every year to put up my fence. It seemed to me that after having traveled and seen something of the world that farming and living a lonely life at the "Dirt Dobber's Nest" was not suited to me. I had no society except a few neighbors married people and sometimes an occasional visit from a friend, perhaps from Suggsville my old home, or elsewhere and my home was quiet lonely. After living there through the first winter, summer came on and a young lady came up from Mobile to visit her relatives at her grandmother's residence who owned a plantation on the river below mine. She came every summer with the balance of her family to rusticate in the country. Her father was a wholesale grocery merchant in Mobile and they were a very nice and clever family. She was quiet pretty and attractive in appearance; vivacious, cheerful, sprightly, and fond or attention as a matter of course. She was fond of horse back riding and I always had a good riding pony for her to ride. We enjoyed ourselves very much in that way. Sometimes we had little "picnics" and fishing parties in the neighborhood. She was quite a recreation for me when she made her annual summer visits to our community.

To hurry up my work I will say that after the expiration of about two years time on the Bigbee with the continued agitation by politicians of the slavery question north and south—the southern states seceded which was considered sufficient cause for war or "casus belli" and war was declared by the United States. We organized the second company of volunteers from our county composed of some of the best material of young men in the county under Captain S. B. Cleveland of Suggsville called the Suggsville Greys. Our last meeting of the company before reporting for service was at Suggsville.

Chapter XV
The War

We had a flag presentation by Miss Emma Portis (daughter of one of our lieutenants) J.W. Portis who did himself credit in making a patriotic speech of encouragement to our men. Captain Cleveland responded in a glowing speech also with great credit to himself in receiving the flag. We took passage on Captain Finnegan's boat at Gosport bound for Mobile. Our company was admitted in the cabin of passengers and got along well except a few who took on too much of the "Queen's eye water" as Doyle, a man in our company, called it.

Doyle was from Grove Hill a printer in the office of Clark County Democrat at that place. He was a man of great wit and humor when drinking late in the night he became thirsty and called for water by asking the cabin boy for the location of the "well," The waiter replied that there was no well on the boat.

He says then, "I will not travel on any boat again unless there is a well on her." But he said "there is no telling what a day may bring forth as Mr. Day said to Mrs. Day."

He said also that he was very hungry and was no musician and could not "play on the fiddle" but always had a fine voice for eating.

Doyle was put in the guard house for drinking. He said that when put in "measles broke out and have broke out of the guard house with them."

When we arrived at Mobile we were mustered into service in the Confederate Army for twelve months about April 1, 1861 and went directly to Fort Morgan where we did military duty and acted as a garrison for the greater part of our time. Our Regiment Second Alabama was drilled at first by Colonel Hardee, afterwards General, and was in a fine state of discipline while he was in command of the post. Harry Maury was elected our Colonel when Hardee was ordered away. We spent our time drilling and standing guard. Our company was sent above "navy cove" once on a scout. Just before our time of service expired we were sent to Fort Pillow in Tennessee above Memphis on the Mississippi river. We were mustered out of service in April 1862 after twelve months time. Part of our regiment reorganized and some of us returned via Memphis. We came down on a very small steamboat the "Little Ben." The battle of Shiloh was fought about ten days after we mustered out.

On arriving in Mobile, I purchased some new clothing and called on my "Sweet heart." She said I looked better after getting rid of surplus flesh in the service which I had put on at the "Dirt Dobber's Nest." In leaving Mobile I went up the Bigbee River to the "Dirt Dobber's Nest" and soon after paid my mother a visit at my Suggsville home. I felt a little relieved from being a soldier and was glad to rest a while for if there is any easy place in the army I have never found it although we had a good time at Fort Morgan. I enjoyed the comforts of "Dirt Dobber's Nest" more than ever before "under my own vine and fig tree" free from military restraint to do and act as I felt disposed at my lonely home in the backwoods of Clark near the Bigbee on Salt Creek.

In the mean time the "Salt works" very near me had been opened and people were coming in numbers to make salt as it was becoming scarce in our country on account of the blockade by the "Yankees." I owned pine land adjacent to the Salt works which was taken from salt water from wells dug there and my mother, brother-in-law, and myself put in some hands to work at the Salt works together in partnership and I furnished the wood for fuel to burn in boiling the water into salt in large kettles made for the purpose. Some of them made at Montgomery Alabama in the iron foundry there to boil salt water into salt. Salt boiled of the water from salt wells was made very fast at the works and at one time it was said a thousand hands were employed and people from different parts of Alabama and Mississippi were engaged in making salt. Salt was worth fifty dollars per bushel and pine wood off the land sold for fifty dollars per acre for fuel for the furnaces. There was three "Salt works" in Clark county, upper, lower, and central works making salt. Money was made fast, but it was confederate money, not worth much. The money was cheap and everything else was high. Meat was worth a dollar a pound and a pair of shoes before the war ended was worth one hundred dollars in confederate money.

As the war was raging our so called government called for more men and feeling it my duty to do so—two of my brothers and myself joined a company which we organized into cavalry under my brother W. P. Barnes as Captain and reported to General Pillow at Montgomery, Alabama who formed a small brigade of two regiments and one battalion of men. We went up into north Alabama and Georgia. The first fight we engaged in was at Lafayette court house in Georgia. The place was garrisoned by Yankees about 400 in number. Our men were dismounted except every fourth man to hold horses and after driving in the pickets about day light one morning we found the enemy blockaded in the court house. Our men advanced on them and in the charge on the court house they killed and wounded several. Our orderly Sergeant and one man were wounded and captured, afterwards died in prison. Major Lewis of our battalion from Cahaba, Alabama was killed. We left the place after the fight was over and while some of our men were made prisoners in the fray, we bought off about sixty Yankees.

46

I left my horse Messenger with the horse holder but in the fight he let them get away. I found a gray mare which belonged to one of our men who did not know where she was. I found him on my horse and I had his nag "Bully for the boy with the glass eye" said I. In the recovery of my horse I lost my six-shooter pistol which I left on the horn of my saddle either lost or stolen; the latter most probably. We were ordered to Tuscaloosa for some cause the "Yankees" raided the town once. General Pillow made a speech at the University building exonerating himself in our late encounter. Some of the college students joined our command as mounted guards on the general's staff.

A small squad of our men were left at Tuscaloosa with jaded and broke down sore back horses and in returning to the command I went by home and procured a fresh horse. His name was Arizona. He came from there.

After the fight at Lafayette, Georgia General Pillow was relieved of his command and we served under Colonel Armistead senior Colonel Of Mississippi regiment. Our command was then called "Armistead's brigade." Colonel Armistead was wounded at Lafayette and I saw him when he came out on his horse from the court house bleeding from a wound in one shoulder. The "Yankees" shot our men from the windows of the court house being blockaded in there and we had no artillery of cannon to dislodge them. Colonel Armistead, I learned, died in a hospital from his wounds in Mississippi after the close of the war.

I think the next fight we engaged in was at Rome, Georgia. The first day we only had a little skirmish fight with the enemy, while Hood's Army marched by going to Tennessee. That night they reinforced on us thinking they were going to fight Hood. We only had our little brigade so called of about four hundred men and one regiment of Texas troops, 9th Texas; all cavalry. We had to fight Kilpatrick's cavalry and the 11th Army Corps. My horse, Arizona, cut his ankle with a cord the night before. I made Hines "my waiting boy" take him to the rear and told him to stay there till after the fight while I rode the mule. I told Hines that he had no better sense and was just fool enough to go to the "Yankees" on my horse. He took me at my word—he did that very thing. I have not seen Hines nor Arizona since. My brother Wilmer lost a negro and horse in the same fight. I hated to lose my horse worse than to lose the negro.

We had to fight against so many that we could only "fire and fallback." They forced us to fallback near the Coosa River and some of our men actually swam their horses across. In fact we got badly worsted and demoralized for they gave us a good beating; "what paddy gave the drum."

After our encounter at Rome, we fell back into Alabama and went to Opelika on our way towards Mobile. We were in many places in Georgia about Dallas, New Hope, and other places where fighting had occurred, but they kept us moving all the while. Our wounded were put in quarters at Gaylesville where I brought my brother Wilmer who was wounded by a blow across the breast with a carbine in the hands of a Yankee in the attempt to knock him off his horse. When we left Opelika we went via Montgomery down the railroad towards Mobile and had an encounter with the enemy who came up to Pollard on a raid from Pensacola. We joined Clanton's brigade to assist them in routing the enemy composed of two or three regiments of negroes and Yankees. They destroyed and burned all the houses and property between Pollard and Bluff Springs on the railroad and killed cattle and hogs on the route.

Our command with Clanton's brigade overtook them late at night after following them all day. The fight commenced in the darkness of night and it did not take long to put them on a retreat for negroes will not stand bullets long. They had wagons loaded with provisions which they scattered all along on the ground to Bluff Springs. Our men fared bountifully next day. We had only three men killed in the fight as they fought behind pine trees for shelter and we did not suffer much loss. The poor fellows who were killed were buried under the pine trees in a lonely country away from kindred and friends. No one seemed to think of them anymore and they were as entirely forgotten as if they had never lived. They were alive the day before in full health, but now forgotten by their comrades in arms. I saw one old negro soldier lying in the road; his head resting on a sack of corn. He had "handed in his checks" and "gone where the woodline twineth" to "Davy Jone's locker" forever.

The weather had become very cold and we went into "winter quarters" at Greenwood below Blakely not far from Perdio River. It was a settlement of nice clever people and we were quite comfortably situated. We sometimes enjoyed dancing with the girls at parties. The girls were always ready for fun; horse back rides, etc. Our men frequently went foraging like all cavalry do. One day two men in same mess concluded to buy some whiskey and bread. They had twenty dollars confederate money between them.

When the fellow returned with it, his messmate inquired of him, "How much did you buy?"

His partner said seventeen dollars and fifty cents worth of whiskey and two dollars and fifty cents in bread!

His mate said, "good gracious Tom what made you buy so much bread?"

Sich is life! We do not know how to be content with our lot.

In the meantime while the war was progressing my sweet-hearts favorite lover came home to Mobile (the one she liked from the beginning, before I ever saw her) and I heard that she was married. "Oh! Ever thus from childhood's hour I have seen my fondest hopes decay I never loved a tree or clover but it was the first to fade away." And I never had a "sweet-heart" that some fellow did not come and take her away. Tis said that a man's heart is like a "crabs claw—break it off and it will sprout again." Mine had been so badly bruised in a previous encounter that I liked her better with my head than with my heart and I came to the conclusion that a confederate soldier had no time to get married. "The oft told take of love's labor lost."

While stationed at Greenwood our service consisted mostly in scouting and one time I was sent towards Pensacola with two men to watch and find out about the movement of the enemy. We went near Pensacola found everything quiet and returned in two or three days. We went one time under Lieutenant Babcock from Cahaba on a scout below the Perdido River leaving our horses on this side; we waded through water part of the time following a guide until day light. We were completely broke down and foundered when we reached our horses on this side of the river where we left them and I could scarcely dismount on reaching our camp at Greenwood.

We went out to meet the "Yankees" one day advancing on Blakely above Fish river and about the time we got into line of battle, Captain Redd who commanded in the absence of higher officers called for a reliable man to go down to Fish River Bridge to relieve some of our men on guard there who would be cut off from us by the enemy who were advancing on us at the time. The task was given to me and as I rode down in sight of the enemy towards the bridge they fired on me two or three times after which four of their cavalry took a stand in the road two of them facing each way. I relieved the men at the bridge and going back to Greenwood we went up to Blakely that night reaching there about daylight we could hear them fighting in the pine woods.

Our command was soon ordered to Mobile. Some of them were in the fight at Spanish Fort. It was thought the enemy would attack Mobile in the rear by land on Dog river—simultaneously with the gun ships in the gulf on Fort Morgan by water—part of our troops went over to Mobile and going out to Spring Hill about six miles, we remained one night and next day we returned to the city. Some of our men were dismounted and left to fight at Blakely; the balance of us marched up into Mississippi to the state line. In the meantime in marching up the Bigbee near by I crossed the river at Jackson after wading and swimming my horse in back water along the road to the ferry. I spent the night with Dr. Denny at Jackson. He gave me a dry pair of socks to put on in the place of the wet ones on my feet. I told him of losing my negro and horse at Rome. He said the "darkies" would all be free before long. It was so, but I hated to lose my horse Arizona. I went home to see my mother on my jaded horse which cost only three thousand dollars in confederate money before at the Salt Works near the Dirt Dobber's Nest, my lonely bachelor home. In the meantime the "Yankees" took Mobile. Some of them were at Claiborne and on the other side of the Alabama River. We were looking for them to come over into Clark County but the river was too high. We thought they would soon overrun our country. One of my mother's carriage horses had been impressed into our army service and she told me I could take the other and all the mules if I wished with me in the army to save them. I took charge of Dock, a fine bay horse, and sent word to the plantation for all the negroes who wished to go in the army with me to come next day and bring a mule to ride. Only one man came on a mule. I bid my mother good bye and crossing the river at Jackson went that night to Bladon Springs enroute for the State Line.

On reaching State Line where I found our command in camp we heard of the surrender of Mobile and in a few days was sent as part of an escort on the train with Captain Shelton and a federal officer on General Canby's staff with orders to Meridian from Mobile. When we arrived at Meridian, I saw Dick Wainwright there who told me that General Lee had surrendered his army in Virginia and the war was at an end. When we returned to our camp at the State Line some of our men said they would not surrender, but mounted their horses and went home—they did surrender anyhow at home. We were marched to Livingston Alabama to get our paroles. "The child was born and his name was Anthony," the "bottom dropped out" and we all went home.

Chapter XVI
Confed's return "lost cause"

It is useless to go over the details of our journey home. We came down from Livingston into Perry county and Marengo into Clarke County home. I was glad the war was over and was willing to submit to the situation and conditions of surrender in the "lost cause" for the sake of peace anyhow. I had some cotton at my place on the Bigbee which was made the first year of the war while I was at Fort Morgan. I hired a white man to take charge of my farm to make a crop. Major Austill a near neighbor and friend sent his hands over and helped out plowing for me as I was a confederate soldier and the crop turned out well. It was strange that no one troubled by cotton which was lying in an out house with the door open and broke down until I had it taken to the gin sometime after the war. It was shipped to Mobile and sold for a good price. I went to Mobile about that time and meeting with many friends had a jolly time. We had been accustomed to spending confederate money free and everything being high after the war greenbacks went the same way and shared the same fate. I was "sowing wild oats" about that time and did not care for expenses nor for anything else. A confederate soldier with whom I happened to meet stole the watch my father gave me. I put him in jail and paid fifty dollars to recover it, turn the man loose and let him go—I have the watch yet.

After settling down to business I concluded to have the old saw mill on my mother's land repaired to saw lumber. The old mill house was there but the dam was gone for as a fellow said in making a pun on words: "you sometimes find a dam by a mill site, but do not always find a mill by a dam site." The mill was there this time but the dam was "nonest" blown up and "gone glimmering through the days that were." I called on "Uncle Ned" the old standby to help me once more he was now a free-man but the same "Old Ned." The water had washed out deep holes below the dam which had to be filled up before it was finished.

I bought a place on a ridge below the ford and mill near Simmons creek called the "Fitts place" which was owned by a man of that name which had a small double log house on it "Uncle Ned" put it in good repair by adding a front piazza to it. Being near Simmons creek and once owned by Fitts, I called it "Fittsimmons." I gave the contract to a man to repair the old saw and grist mill. He and another man stayed with me at "Fittsimmons" and finished the work in about three months. The saw and grist mill did well until the end of the year after which my hands went back on the farms. I went to the old plantation to plant corn and cotton again. Our negroes did well as free labor, most of them being our old slaves on the place.

I bought a fine young horse from my oldest brother Dr. J. P. Barnes who went back to Mobile after the war closed. His name was Beauregard. I took a notion one day to plant some corn for Beauregard and to plow it myself. He was not used to plowing—neither was I, for I do not think that I was cut out for a "plowboy" if so I was "spoilt in the making" some may call it laziness "I deny the allegation and defy the alligator," for I took Beauregard and put him to the plow. He was my saddle horse. He would try to leave the corn field at the end of every row going towards home. It made me drink water. I got sick with fever. I did not plow the corn any more but overlooked the hands employed on the plantation after that.

The next year I rented the "Beaver Ruin" plantation—made a good crop—could not get good labor on the place, sold my "Bigbee" farm—went to Texas bought a drove of Texas horses—put my money in a store—let other men manage—lost it—went into a store at Jackson—had to give up my place to a brother of the proprietor—went to Wilcox county after my mother was too old to keep house—was agent for a picture company—took pictures myself—I afterwards went into business with an old friend Dr. Callier at Chadwick, Alabama. Here I met a lady from Talladega on a visit to her brother.

She became my wife after I had "lost all save honor." We were married January 7, 1886. We went via Selma down the Alabama on a visit to my relatives in south Alabama after which we arrived at her residence in Talladega in the winter of 1886. We went out to "Shocco Springs" a summer resort which belonged to my wife with the object of taking boarders. It proved to be too wet and rainy in the summer season which prevented us from doing much in the way of boarders. We moved back to her home in town. We rented and leased "Shocco Springs" off and on for several years. Before our marriage my wife lost her rent on "Shocco Springs" by renting to parties who were not responsible and after making a years living out of it they had nothing to pay rent. I did a little better than that, but nothing to brag on. I sold books and was local agent for nursery stock while in Talladega. I rented a stove and engaged in retail grocery trade for three years, but gave up the business for want of capital. I went back to my nursery business while I lived in Talladega.

Talladega is a lovely place of about six thousand inhabitants black and white situated in the base and is called the "bride of the mountains." The inhabitants are intelligent, thrifty, and progressive. I can truly say that the fifteen years of my married life with my good and kind-hearted wife was the happiest part of my life while living at Talladega. She was all I wished her to be, not having the advantages of an early liberal education, but my attachment for her was sincere and affectionate. She was my best and truest friend, my bosom companion; she was my poor suffering wife!

Her health failed and for more than twelve months she suffered intensely. Our family physician did all in his power to relieve her suffering and pain during her illness at home. We lived on Battle Street which takes its name from the battle fought with the Indians on that street in the war of 1812-1813. They fought down Battle Street by the big spring on Spring Street (which now supplies the town with water) to Isbell's farm near the furnace. My mother's' father, my grandfather, William Patterson, a merchant from Savannah, Georgia who was in command of a company of cavalry under Floyd in General Jackson's army was in the fight on battle street where we lived in Talladega, Alabama over one hundred years after. Mrs. Thompson's husband, my wife's mother-in-law by first marriage, was in the same fight.

FITTSIMMONS.

Chapter XVII
"My Wife"

To make a painful subject to me as brief as possible I will say that my poor wife continued to suffer from ill health and our family physician, Dr. Simms, with others decided that a surgical operation would be necessary. She was taken to Dr. Brown's hospital in Birmingham Alabama where he performed the difficult and dangerous operation July 4, 1901. After remaining there two weeks, I brought her back home to Talladega where she suffered until death came to her relief after about three and a half months illness and intense pain—October 23, 1901. She has gone to the spirit land. Her soul took flight to the God who gave it. She sleeps in the city cemetery in the city of the dead at Talladega. She is now my angel wife! She said she hated to leave me, but was resigned to her fate. It was her dying request that I should not grieve. Let the curtain drop and the bitter cup pass for I am weeping while I write.

I left a home in Talladega which was hers during her life time, but mine no more, with a heavy broken heart. I went to Selma to see a relative—my good kind-hearted niece—for whom I shall always entertain a fond remembrance and attachment. She was kind to me in my troubles. The good book says "whom the Lord loveth, he chasteneth." I am satisfied that my troubles which have been inflicted upon me were sent for my own good and betterment for verily, "I am a man of sorrows and acquainted with grief" and feel that I am a better man in the sight of God, my creator. After remaining in Selma a short while with my niece, Mrs. Portis, I accepted an invitation from my old friend and companion in my youth and early manhood Dr. Callier at Chadwick, Perry County, Alabama who came in a conveyance to take me out to his quiet home in the country. I had left him just seventeen years previous a happy married man, but sad to say returned to the same place with crape on my hat!

Dr. Callier and myself had known each other in our halcyon days as he calls it, before we had ever known that trouble was or in our "antebellum" days when we had what we wanted without any trouble at all, Not so now, for we have undergone a severe ordeal of "Yankee treatment" since the war, at one time our plantations joined. He had a pony called Red Bug and my pony was named Cricket. One day Cricket and Red Bug got frightened in the road at something and tried to run away with us. He says I remarked that our ponies were making fools of themselves "trying to act like horses; like the pig, making a hog of himself."

I remained at Chadwick with my friend Dr. Callier for several months bemoaning the loss by death of the best gift to mortal man on earth; my poor suffering wife. She has gone forever as she said to that "beautiful shore" where none but angels go and where I hope to meet her again in a "house not made with hands eternal in the Heavens" around the throne of God. I received an invitation about the first of the year 1903 from my relatives at Dry Fork, Wilcox County, Alabama to come to live with them and I arrived here where I am writing this book on January 7, 1903 just seventeen years from the date of my marriage at Chadwick in 1886. I was here then on a bridal tour, but now, alone in the world.

I feel it my duty to state that my wife whose maiden name was Anna Chadwick was born in Raleigh, North Carolina, February 5, 1843. She lived in Perry County Alabama where her father owned a farm after which the family went to Selma where she was first married to Jarrett Thompson of Talladega, Alabama. She was on a visit to her brother at Chadwick where we were married in 1886. Her brother's name was John Chadwick after whom the post office was named. Her father was killed at Vicksburg during the siege by a bullet through a port hole from a gun in the hands of a sharp shooter. She has only one brother left, Thomas L. Chadwick who is living with Dr. Callier at Chadwick in Perry County.

(217) DRY FORK, 1903

Chapter XVIII
Dry Fork

D ry Fork is the name of the old family home built by Captain James A. Tait about seventy years ago. It is a true type of old time "antebellum" southern planter's home. It was built of fine material of solid wood and stands well the test of time. Captain Tait at the time of his death was no doubt the wealthiest planter in Wilcox County Alabama where he lived. He left his several sons and daughters in affluence before the war.

"Dry Fork" with two plantations one on either side the river with ferry and warehouse at "Blacks Bluff" was bequeathed to his youngest son and namesake James G. Tait whose first wife was my sister Adele and his second wife, my niece, was Miss Amelia Barnes of Mobile. I am staying with them. The room which I am occupying now was the apartment in which his grandfather Judge Tait of Georgia fame died. Southern hospitality as in "antebellum" days as I said before is a thing of the past and although the old southern planters heart is in the same and right place as in former days, he has not the ability or time to devote to entertainment of friends however willing he might be property has decreased in value, labor is free and not so reliable since the war. Mr. Tait lost one plantation by security debt after the war and although he owns about three thousand acres yet, he says his tax assessment is only about ten thousand now instead of one hundred and eighty-five thousand in slavery times. He will utilize a part of his farm in future to stock raising.

I had made an application at one time since the death of my wife, having no children, to gain admittance as an inmate to the "Soldiers home" in Alabama, but it seems the state did not help them this time and they can accommodate but a few only yet. "Pity the sorrows of a poor old man, whose trembling limbs have borne him to your door." Pity the homeless confederate the only living memento of a forlorn hope and a "lost cause."

"Uncle Ned" moved to his cabin on the road to the plantation near my mother's home with his last wife, Margaret, after the death of "Aunt Penny" where he died a few years after the war. You will see in the picture of his cabin that he has laid down

De shubble and de hoe
Dere was an old nigga des called "Uncle Ned"

He's dead long ago, long ago
He had no wool on the top of his head
The place where de wool ought to grow
Den lay down de shubble and de hoe
Hang up de fiddle and de bow
No mo hand work for poor "old Ned"
He's gone whar de good niggas go."

Peace to the ashes of my father's old faithful slave and God bless! His poor old honest soul where I hope to meet him in another world.

(217)　DRY FORK, 1903.

Chapter XIX
Conclusion

I am writing hurriedly to avoid being tiresome and monotonous. I have neglected to mention some things which ought to have been observed. In the death of our Major Lewis, of Cahaba, Alabama our battalion was commanded by major W. V. Harrell now of Talladega county who proved to be a brave and efficient officer. I notice that the major and John Warwick have just received their confederate crosses of honor on Memorial Day at Talladega, Alabama where they both reside. I will also mention the death of Lieutenant Frank Walker of Dallas County who was killed while guarding a bridge on the Montgomery and Mobile railroad not far from canoe station where we camped before going to our winter quarters at Greenwood. Lieutenant Walker rode a fine dapple gray horse which came to camp without his rider with nothing to show save his bridle and saddle and our men concluded he was killed by a detachment of negro troops at the bridge. J. K. Weisinger near Talladega Alabama was also a member of Lewis battalion. Lieutenant Walker had a brother John Walker in the same company. They were both brave soldiers.

It is strange what changes will take place sometimes in the course of man's natural existence and sojourn on earth and I can only compare it with the revolutions of the wheel of our "little overshot mill" while one bucket fills with water going up the other spills and waste on the ground going down. The wheel of fortune has changed with me and I have had my ups and downs in life and although I have seen "better days" it has been predicted that the balance of my days will be prosperous and happy "So note it be"—There is a divinity that shapes our ends." And "never grieve after spilt milk, but grab up your milk hail and go for the next cow," if there is one left in the pen.

Success

"Tis the coward who quits to misfortune
Tis the knave who changes each day
Tis the fool who wins half the battle
Then throws all his chances away.

There is little in life but labor

And tomorrow may find that a dream;
Success is the bride of endeavor
And luck—but a meteor's gleam.

The time to succeed when others
Discourage, show traces of tive;
The battle is fought in the homestretch
And won—twixt the flag and the wire."

John Trotwood Moore

The reader will please excuse me for neglecting to mention a few lit-tle things which I wish included in the make up of my book—for instance I have said that my father made a codicil to his will in which he gave me his watch, pony, and gun. The watch was made to order in England by a Mr. Johnson when I was a small boy. It has had two mishaps—first stolen in Mobile but was recovered. It was in a merchant's safe in Talladega which fell from a floor into the cellar during a fire several years ago! Receiving a severe jar. It is running in good order now. The picture of my pony Cricket was taken at Suggsville in front of the Female Academy. The gun is with my nephew and namesake F. M. Tait near Dry Fork. It was once stolen also from the overseer house at the plantation when the overseer had several negroes in the woods run away. My father gave orders that if the gun was not returned every negro on the plantation would be punished. He found it one night soon afterwards sitting inside the yard gate. The gun, watch, and picture of my pony Cricket is all I have left of his estate.

Strange to say that he gave me this property thinking that I was a steady boy and would take care of it. I have done so up to date. The gun in question has been the death of many of the American deer found in "antebellum" days and hunted by your humble servant in days gone by in the pine woods of Clark county Alabama.

In making mention of my school days in Selma Alabama at the Masonic Institute in 1849-1850, I forgot to say that I boarded with Dr. Lavender on Broad Street at that time the principal street of the town. My classmates in Latin were Dick Jones, William (Bill) Horn, and Lewis Bayne under Professor Lowery; a fine teacher. Dick Jones married a daughter of Dr. Neal Smith of Clark County. She became Mrs. Rixey after his death. I met Billy Horn in Texas at Bastrop in 1856. He said he had a writing school at the time, but had acted on the stage, drove cattle, and done everything out there for a living. I saw Lewis Bayne in his drug store at Selma in winter of 1901. He did not know me of course both being old men and had not met in fifty years.

There are many little incidents which happened during our war too trifling to be mentioned in history. Among other things our little command was compelled to forage on our people for feed for our horses. We would often march all day long going from one section of the country to another and arriving at a place to camp would rid a mile or two to some house for corn at night made by women and children whose husbands and fathers were in our army. One time we went to a poor woman's house for corn at night. She had only a rail pen full enough only to feed our horses that night. It was all she had to bread her family. Our men filled their wallets. I paid her in confederate money for mine. They gave her on order on our government for the corn but I venture to say that the money I gave her (which did not supply the place of corn) was all she received for her hard earnings that night.

My mother while her sons were in the army fighting for the "Lost Cause" gave corn to poor women and children in Clark County Alabama; families of men fighting in our army whenever they came to her for help "Small favors thankfully received" at the time perhaps but I venture to say that the recipients of such kindness in time of need, bordering on starvation, do not thank my mother who sleeps in her grave at the old "homestead" for past favors thinking she only did her duty in contributing to their wants.

As I have said before I have "my ups and downs" like the Irishman's frog, "when he stands up he sits down and when he walks he goes by fits and starts" and it might be best to take it "slow and steady to win the race" like the "tortoise" which he calls the "walking snuff box" but not go too fast like the railroad car which the Irishman has also given the name of "hell in harness" and the reader would not believe that an old man like me who has past the "three score and ten" mile post and one who has not mounted a horse in fifteen years past could ride fifty miles in a first days travel to my youngest brother's home.

Mrs. English, his wife's mother, was a sister of General George B. McCellan of Philadelphia well known to fame in the United States. I have two brothers living at Suggsville, Clark County Alabama. I have only one sister living at Barlow Bend Clark County. Her husband R. H. Flinn is also a cotton planter on the Alabama River. My two brothers at Suggsville were late Alfred Y. and Dr. B. S. Barnes. My brothers like myself who are living have lost their wives, but they have interesting families of children and grandchildren who are fighting the "battle of life." I am proud of my family relations and my greatest ambition in my declining years is to be prosperous and happy; free from want in this world and that we all may meet again to gather around the throne of grace in a "House not made with hands eternal in the Heavens, where the wicked cease from troubling and the weary are at rest."

I have been to see once more after the expiration and lapse of several years of time the old family home to behold for the first time my mother's grave. I also saw once more the spot where Uncle Ned's cabin stood. It has been replaced by a new one. He has "laid down the shovel and the hoe; hung up the fiddle and the bow and has gone where the good niggers go."

THE END

MATERNAL CARE.

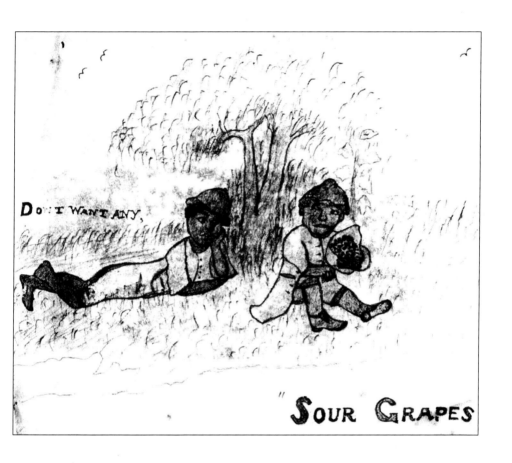

AUNT PENNY.

(66)

(219.)

North — "Kalina;" RAZOR-BACK, "AT HALF MAST."

RACE-
-PROBLEM,
SETTLED.
POSSUM
HUNT.
POSSUM SOP, AND-
BAKE PERTATER,
Johnny dont you
mention it.
(Page 59.)

LITTLE PET.

FLAT BOAT EXPLOSION.

OLD WASH
(Carpenter.)

OLD "BLAZE" AND THE DEER.
(HARWELL GOODWIN.)

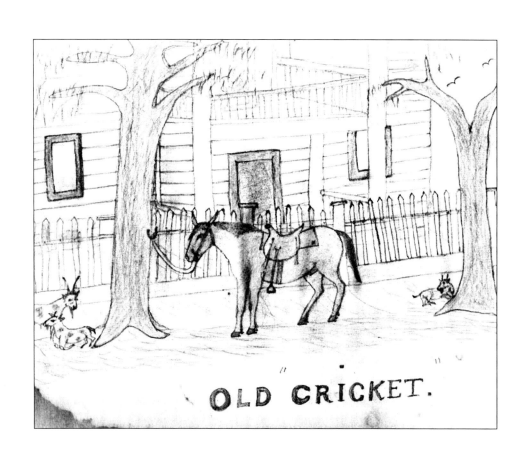

"OLD" CRICKET.

CONFED'S RETURN—"LOST CAUSE"— DESERTED HOME.

(Page 201.) (over)

MRS MALONYS PIG.

45 Ft. Dillon
46 LAFAYETE Couhu
47 Col Armisted died
47 Rome
48 Turnay
49 Blackewy
49 Spanish Fort
Yh Sealy Hill
50 Livingston